D0062654

MY FATHER
AND OTHER WORKING-CLASS
FOOTBALL HEROES

Gary Imlach started out writing for national newspapers at the age
of eighteen. He has worked for the BBC, ITN, CNN and Channel 4,
and he presents ITV's coverage of the Tour de France and American
Football. He is also the producer of several documentaries. This is
his first book.

JW
_____

Happy Birthday 2013
Forty years I have
known you
wow !!
Love

MY FATHER
AND OTHER
WORKING-CLASS
FOOTBALL HEROES

Gary Imlach

YELLOW JERSEY PRESS
LONDON

Published by Yellow Jersey Press 2006

13 15 17 19 20 18 16 14

Copyright © Gary Imlach 2005

Gary Imlach has asserted his right under the
Copyright, Designs and Patents Act 1988 to be identified
as the author of this work

This book is sold subject to the condition that it shall not,
by way of trade or otherwise, be lent, resold, hired out
or otherwise circulated without the publisher's prior
consent in any form of binding or cover other than that
in which it is published and without a similar condition
including this condition being imposed on the
subsequent purchaser

First published in Great Britain in 2005 by
Yellow Jersey Press

Yellow Jersey Press
Random House, 20 Vauxhall Bridge Road,
London SW1V 2SA

Random House Australia (Pty) Limited
20 Alfred Street, Milsons Point, Sydney,
New South Wales 2061, Australia

Random House New Zealand Limited
18 Poland Road, Glenfield,
Auckland 10, New Zealand

Random House South Africa (Pty) Limited
Isle of Houghton, Corner of Boundary Road & Carse O'Gowrie,
Houghton, 2198, South Africa

Random House Publishers India Private Limited
301 World Trade Tower, Hotel Intercontinental Grand Complex,
Barakhamba Lane, New Delhi 110 001, India

The Random House Group Limited Reg. No. 954009
www.randomhouse.co.uk

A CIP catalogue record for this book
is available from the British Library

ISBN 9780224072687

The Random House Group Limited supports The Forest Stewardship
Council (FSC®), the leading international forest certification organisation.
Our books carrying the FSC label are printed on FSC® certified paper. FSC
is the only forest certification scheme endorsed by the leading
environmental organisations, including Greenpeace. Our paper procurement
policy can be found at www.randomhouse.co.uk/environment

Typeset by Palimpsest Book Production Limited,
Polmont, Stirlingshire

Printed and bound by
CPI Group (UK) Ltd, Croydon, CR0 4YY

Contents

Prologue:
Memorabilia

WHAT WERE MY CHANCES of finding him in here?
The Galleon Suite of the Royal National Hotel in Bloomsbury didn't look immediately promising – perhaps a hundred trestle tables overflowing with the results of a hopelessly imprecise search-engine query: football, the past.

The Silver Jubilee edition of the Giant New Year Programme Fair was being held on what would have been my father's seventieth birthday. It had seemed like too much of a coincidence to pass up when I'd seen it advertised, an apt way to mark the milestone that death had deprived him of by a few months. Now, though, I was feeling an almost pre-match tightening of the stomach. I wanted to reassure myself that he was here, alive and well in posterity among the community of the collected.

It was a large and catholic community: programmes; pennants; Ronaldo phonecards; a picture-disc single of Kevin Keegan singing in German; Eusebio posed in a series of photographs with celebrities from around the world; fourteen home-made Arsenal scrapbooks covered in brown paper.

And here were the collectors' cards, telling their head-shot history of the game as sold and swapped down the decades. Cigarette stars of the '20s in their arms-folded, portrait-studio formality, the hand-coloured post-war heroes of *The Wizard* and *The Hotspur*, the soft perms of the '70s. Malcolm Macdonald and Trevor Francis were there in 3-D, their skin tones strangely rendered, as though some period polyester had infiltrated the photographic reproduction process.

There was a smell — damp garages and back bedrooms — not all of which could be accounted for by the merchandise. The dealers and their customers, interchangeable for the most part, had the look of men banished from the parts of their homes accessible to visitors. I felt like an impostor at a secret-society reunion, lacking the necessary passwords and arcane knowledge. At the stalls enquiries were made less out of a genuine intention to buy than the urge to display a greater familiarity with the item on offer than the person selling it. Historical facts were vouchsafed. There was banter of a sort.

'Back again, eh?'

''77–78, I'm sure of it . . .'

'No I'm telling you, '78–79.'

'Are you doing Potters Bar on the 20th?'

These were men (there was the occasional wife or glum daughter) bonding over a century of soccer history. And progressively happier the further back into it they went.

'We used to get these European Cup Final programmes in the '70s and you'd struggle to get pennies for them,' one stallholder reminisced.

'Yeah, no one was interested then.'

'Remember when it was still fun to go to the games, before we got promoted?'

In front of one stall, a photographer was posing an old boy with his purchase.

'And I'll be in *Four by Two* magazine, will I?'

'That's right mate, *FourFourTwo*.'

The magazine itself had already passed into the realms of the collectible: one stall was selling back copies from 1999. Another customer was explaining his particular interests to a Belgian dealer who had a selection of postcards featuring the football grounds of Europe: 'I like the aerial views.' Then, fearing incomprehension, 'VIEW AH-RIEL,' pronounced in the Continental manner.

The past here seemed to be not so much another country as a garden shed in the suburbs. Surely this wasn't a love of football, just nostalgia and a love of collecting, which chance or childhood might as easily have pointed towards model trains or Northern Soul. I felt the need for some fresh air. But first I had to find my dad.

It wasn't as though I'd never seen any evidence of his career. There was a trunk full of it in my parents' attic, stuff that nothing on display in the Galleon Suite could touch. We used to haul it down regularly when we were kids. Later, less often, on return trips home. There was his Scotland shirt from the 1958 World Cup and his Nottingham Forest FA Cup Final kit from the following year: red V-neck cotton shirt with white trim; white silk shorts with red piping; red-topped white socks; white tracksuit for the walk out of the tunnel, with a zip pocket at the breast embroidered in red – NFFC Wembley 1959. There was his winner's medal.

In the year before my father died, someone had sent him a cutting from the Nottingham *Evening Post*. One of his teammates was selling his medal anonymously at auction, embarrassed perhaps to share the circumstances that had brought about the sale. Another item from the trunk in the attic held a possible explanation. *The Forest Cup Story* was the official souvenir magazine published in the weeks before the final, and the centre pages were given over to profiles of the players. Along with the usual litany of family details, hobbies and favourite food, each man was asked about his post-football career plans. Chic Thomson, Goalkeeper: *probably a return to the dry-cleaning business, building machines*; Bob McKinlay, Centre-Half: *training to be a motor mechanic*; Tommy Wilson, Centre-Forward: *to become a shop-keeper*; Stewart Imlach, Outside-Left: *a return to the joinery business.*

My father and his teammates came from the same stock as those who packed the terraces every week to watch them. And they knew they were heading back into that community when their playing days were over – perhaps more accurately, had never really left. Any of them with foresight enough to see the ephemera of their jobs as the venerated relics of a future global cult could, by now, have been making a killing on the memorabilia circuit.

As I walked around I recognised a few items from home. The *1959 FA Cup Final* programme was priced at £25, the *1958 World Cup Tournament* brochure £350. There were commemorative postcards featuring each of the Swedish host cities, the kind of thing my father might have sent home: 'Hello Love, Just a few lines . . .' There were first-day covers too. I bought one for my mother. It was all circumstantial evidence, though. I was after the man himself.

I finally found him among the collectors' cards, part of a series by a German company. '*Im Londoner Wembley-Stadion ein volles Haus (100,000 Zuschauer!),*' read the caption on the back. ' *. . . konnte die Mannschaft von Nottingham Forest den Pokal durch einen 2:1-Erfolg über Luton Town erringen.*'

On the front, the hand-tinted figure of my father stands in profile in the Royal Box. Ahead of him Jack Burkitt, the Forest Captain, is holding aloft an unfeasibly yellow FA Cup for the grinning approval of the Duke of Edinburgh. Behind him his teammates are lining up to do what my father will do in just a few seconds: shake the gloved hand of a youthful Queen Elizabeth and accept his medal.

What had that moment been like for him? Why didn't I know? Why had I never asked him this simple question? In fact, how had I managed to let him die without properly gathering together the details of his career, his life story?

It should have been there that the reproaches rained down on me, standing in a room full of the packaged past. The realisation that there was probably a Forest fanatic at one of the stalls, some Scottish football completist, one of the milling, trainspotting crowd I'd been so dismissive of, who had a better grasp of my father's career than I did. Thoughts of how I'd relied on the items in the attic instead of sitting down and talking to him. How the edited highlights and their supporting props had come to stand for his whole career.

But as I stood there holding his picture in its protective plastic sleeve none of this occurred to me. All I was thinking about was not subjecting the old man to the indignity of haggling for him. I paid the asking price and left.

Chapter One
Son of

MAY 2ND 1959 TO MARCH 12TH 1960. Ten months, however much you squint at the calendar. It was close, but no Man of the Match cigar. Apparently I couldn't trace my origins back to a room at the Savoy, hadn't been the result of a joyous, post-cup final victory celebration. Almost, but not quite.

Around the age of twelve or thirteen, once I was old enough to make the tentative connection, I'd tried stretching the facts, cooking the biology books. Discovering that the human gestation period was forty weeks, not thirty-six, had been a breakthrough; the realisation that lunar months weren't their calendar equivalents a deflating setback.

I was born on a Saturday. There was a minute's silence at the City Ground before kick-off. A few hours after I'd arrived the Forest President George Cottee had definitively departed, buried in a service thoughtfully arranged to give the mourners plenty of time to be in their seats before three o'clock. During *Sports Parade* on the BBC's Light Programme, Eamonn Andrews gave both events a mention in his build-up to the afternoon's football coverage. By the time the news had ricocheted through kitchen windows, over garden fences and off the houses, untouched by telephone wires, of the estate in Bury where my mother's parents lived, they were being congratulated on the arrival of their first granddaughter. Football, media, misrepresentation; here was a child destined to grow up into a sloppy sports journalist. Forest, playing in black armbands, went down 3–1 at home to Spurs.

The Cup Final connection was too much of a good story to let go of completely, though, the idea that I could retrospectively place myself into the defining day of my family football history in a sort of embryo-cameo role. Perhaps it was part of trying to compensate for the fact that I'd never really seen my dad play, or had the chance to play with him. The only exceptions were the charity matches he regularly appeared in after he retired.

For a young boy just coming to terms with the game these could be confusing affairs to get a handle on. Were they serious, or just Sunday kickabouts? (Both.) Wasn't it against the rules for a player to change sides after ten minutes? (Depends how famous you are.) Who was that out-of-breath fat man? (Difficult to say: could be an ex-international centre-half who'd since opened a pub, or one of the organisers intent on kicking a big name before high blood pressure forced him off at half-time.)

My father enjoyed these matches enormously, but in earnest. I remember him being astonishingly fast; he seemed to be competing in a different kind of game altogether from some of the more languid ex-players, many of them quite a bit younger than he was. One thing puzzled me: as he ran his jaw seemed to be yanked open with every stride, as if it were invisibly attached to one knee. It was almost as though the standard mechanics of air intake couldn't provide the oxygen demanded by his sheer relentlessness, and so he had to scoop up extra as he went, snapping down the wing like a crocodile. It was fascinating to watch, and must have mesmerised the odd full-back in his playing days. He himself was unaware of it and completely uncurious when it was pointed out. A shrugged 'Oh?' was all my mother got out of him on the subject, and we never discovered either the cause or the effect. If it was part of his internal combustion process it worked. Before his joints stopped him running altogether, he stayed fast and fit through middle age. In fact, with the cruel exception of his last two years when disease took the matter out of his hands, he cut exactly the same figure through decades of family and newspaper photographs: short, trim, feet at ten-to-two, carrying no more excess weight than a ballet dancer.

Steve, my older brother, would take his boots and sometimes got a game, or part of a game, in place of one of the advertised ex-pros who was still at home nursing a hangover, or had forgotten the vague commitment he'd made months ago in some players' lounge or other after a match. Almost as often, Steve got on as a substitute when my father's knee locked and he had to be helped off grimacing. We were used to the sight. It happened regularly, although less heroically, at home when he bent forward to switch channels on the television — a legacy of the incomplete cartilage surgery which had signalled the slow end of his playing career in the early '60s.

On the stretch of living-room wall between the TV set in the corner and my father's armchair next to the music-centre hung his Cup Final mementoes, three framed items in flying-duck formation. There was a photograph of him shaking hands with the Duke of Edinburgh before the game — 'Another bloody Scot!' — one of him receiving his medal from the Queen afterwards, and between them the medal itself, set into a square of dark velvet.

They'd been a decorative constant against the changing wallpaper of half a dozen club houses since 1959: Nottingham, Luton, Coventry, Crystal Palace, back to Nottingham and on to Everton. These last two stops were coaching jobs, first as assistant manager at Notts County under Billy Gray, his old inside-left from the Forest cup-winning team, then at Harry Catterick's School of Science, in charge of the youth sides to begin with, then working his way up to first-team coach.

Later, when he moved on to Blackpool and Bury, the photos and the medal stayed put, my mother finally having tired of packing them and the rest of the contents of the house every couple of years and recreating family life in a new town, with new neighbours, new schools and the long list of responsibilities that fell to her because my father was busy fulfilling his responsibilities to football.

Eventually the cup final display, in its unfashionable diagonal, had to come down. My father had been pictured in the papers standing in front of it, and there'd been a couple of recent break-ins along the street. The medal went in a drawer in my parents' bedroom with his penknives and golf tees, the pictures rejoined the rest of his career in the attic. By then my brothers and I were busy with the gruelling work of being sullen teenagers, and years of familiarity had made the three small squares and their contents almost invisible. Still, their sudden disappearance from the fixtures and fittings of family life registered as a loss.

For a nine-year-old newly arrived on Merseyside in 1969, though, there was more kudos in having a current member of the Everton coaching staff for a father than a cup-winner from before I was born. Formby is a small coastal town on the way north to Southport, still a popular spot for Everton and Liverpool players who don't fancy the posher parts of the Wirral. We'd been parachuted in that summer as marked men. Our footballing heritage was very much a sidebar to the big news that we were Goodison insiders; something our school friends could go home and ask their dads about, if they remembered.

Besides, our father's achievements were all safely in the record books. We took pride in them, but there was nothing we could do to influence the outcome of games already played and trophies long since held aloft on open-top buses. The '69–70 League Championship, though, was up for grabs, and we knew we had to do our bit. The same clothes every week, the scarf on the same way, the standing and shouting of exactly the same phrase of exhortation to the defence every time Everton conceded a corner: who knew what variables might affect the result one way or the other? Best to cover all the bases just to be on the safe side.

This was part of the responsibility that came with what, across the playground, must have looked like tremendous privilege. At school the only other football offspring our age were the children of the Liverpool centre-half Ron Yeats, and they were girls. So, alone among our peers, we had the secret knowledge. We knew what cars they drove, what their training numbers were, what they ate before matches. When Alan Ball signed a contract with a Danish company no one had heard of and became the first English player to wear white boots it was big news – all our mates were talking about it. But we knew something else: that Alan Ball didn't actually like his new boots and rarely wore them; that his highly visible Hummel were, in fact, usually a pair of Adidas 2000 with a fresh coat of Dulux. We'd seen them. Our dad had painted them. We had a pair of his stiff and creaky Hummel rejects hanging up in the garage for any friends who didn't believe us.

In retrospect, half a dozen seasons edit down into one endlessly looping football-themed episode of *Jim'll Fix It*. Here we are at the training ground, matching famous faces to their flash cars; struggling to respond to the sudden, unexpected attention of an England international saying hello, making a joke we don't understand; then playing on the same five-a-side pitch the first-team squad has just vacated, kicking the same balls, dyed orange by the all-weather surface.

And here's the match-day sequence of us arriving at Goodison Park: pulling past the onlookers into the officials-only car park; out of the car, past the autograph hunters, across the pitch and down the tunnel to the players' lounge for sandwiches and Sam Leitch's *Football Preview*; at the table next to us, Ball, Harvey and Kendall, the finest trio of midfield wives in the country; players themselves suddenly appearing, worryingly close to kick-off, and switching channels to check the racing results; impossibly famous faces, made more unreal by their framing of collars and kipper ties, instead of the crew-necked royal blue in which they'd soon be emerging from the tunnel to the protestant-marching-beat-in-mufti of the *Z-Cars* theme. Here's Freddie Starr, wild-eyed and panting from the warm-up room, lifting his shirt and sweat-printing the shape of his back onto the blue leatherette of every chair in the lounge.

Jack the doorman, Sid the groundsman, Dick the kitman, Jean in the office. Nods, jokes, secret passwords; we were in. We knew all the insiders and the insiders seemed to know us, so it followed that we had to be insiders ourselves. And since they were all performing crucial yet invisible work for the greater glory of the club, surely we were too. The impression was reinforced by the route we took to our seats. The main entrance to the players' lounge was via a corridor that led to the dressing rooms and the tunnel. On the wall opposite there was an unmarked blue door, which opened directly onto the public gangway, just beyond the turnstiles under the main stand.

It was an almost *Alice in Wonderland* moment, a single step that took us from the making-of documentary into the feature film itself; out of the plush privilege of the inner sanctum straight into the coursing mass of fans funnelling towards the concrete stairs and the light at the top of them. There'd be a moment's pause for adjustment – turned heads, quizzical looks from the paying public at three slightly self-conscious kids materialising out of the very fabric of Goodison Park – before we were dissolved into the swell.

Around us in the complimentary seats up towards the back of the stand there was a changing cast of characters. In football's hierarchy of the hanger-on the serious players would be in the directors' box, or possibly in jail. One of the neighbours I regularly turned to, arms raised, to embrace after a goal, I interviewed a few years later in his weekday role as Merseyside's Chief Probation Officer.

It's a trick of memory I know, but I recall the sequence over the PA system that championship season as being the same every week, a liturgy permanently stuck on a single feast day in the calendar: 'Yester-me, Yester-you, Yesterday' by Stevie Wonder; 'Melting Pot' by Blue Mink; the team changes; . . . a big hand please for the Toffee Lady; . . . could the owner of the blue Ford Escort . . . Repetition, superstition. Like brides, the teams were never seen before the ceremonial music started. No coming out half dressed to puncture the anticipation and kill the mystery, no warming up half an hour before kick-off, nothing. And really, nothing was the perfect build-up. Time passing, the ground filling, nervous stomachs synchronising themselves with the stadium clock. Build-ups can't be orchestrated, they build themselves, according to their own rules.

A barely measurable instant before the teams came out below our seats, the news would be signalled across to us by a stirring in the stand opposite. And then the noise would begin. Not a roar as it's usually described, not the involuntary shout of release that a goal produces either, but a great welling up of hope and anticipation, with an undertone of apprehension, what Don DeLillo calls 'longing on a large scale'. And within that large-scale longing, thousands of individuals readying themselves to perform the detailed sequence of devotions they know are somehow crucial to the success of the team.

So, the clothes, the scarf, the standing and shouting of exactly the same phrase to the defence every time Everton conceded a corner (I can't bring myself to divulge it even now). It was a big job for a nine-year-old, all pressure and no power. Failure to adhere precisely to the various rituals in all their nuance could leave me at fault for disaster – a goal against. Doing everything right was no guarantee that the worst wouldn't happen anyway. The season progressed in a series of stomach lurches and heart leaps. The record actually shows that Everton lost just one home game on their way to the league title, but I remember it as a season shot through with potential danger. Perhaps I made a difference.

After the match – more precisely, after a win – the pendulum swung back from responsibility to ridiculous privilege. In the players' lounge the scale-model figures we'd been watching from the stand loomed life-sized and star-shaped; damp hair, loosely knotted ties, drinks in hand. We ticked them off like bubblegum-card collectors. Once we'd completed the set, we knew that meant the dressing rooms must be empty. Short of being in there with the players immediately before the match, which was a perk beyond the scope of our imaginations, being in the dressing room afterwards was about as good as it got. As long as Dick hadn't cleaned up.

Tie-ups, wristbands, mud moulded into the shape of six-pack plastic on the bottoms of boots, stray studs, team-sheets. These were items not available in the club shop, Imlach exclusives, evidence. It wasn't enough just to get in, we needed something we could carry back with us across the dividing line to the world where the rest of our friends lived.

After a while we knew what to expect from the home dressing room. For one thing, there'd always be a scattering of half-read match programmes, which to me were a puzzling disappointment. Programmes were what we read in the stands to kill the time before kick-off because we had nothing more glamorous to do, like being actual players. The image of the players themselves having a quiet flick through, one eye on the dressing-room clock, wasn't the kind of inside information I was keen on gathering. The visitors', though, always held the promise of a really big find. It generally had the look of a hastily abandoned hotel room; the guests, late for the airport, jettisoning stuff they couldn't be bothered to pack, and too pushed for time to check that they hadn't forgotten anything. We were the dishonest cleaning staff.

In truth most of the available booty was usually medical: strapping, rolls of bandage that we'd take home for tie-ups. Once, when Leeds United, at the height of their elegant thuggery, began wearing numbered stocking tabs – perhaps they did a leg count after the game to make sure they hadn't come off the field with anybody else's – my brother picked up a complete set off the floor of the away dressing room. Their next appearance was during the Wednesday afternoon games period at Formby High – *Look, they've got Velcro on the back to keep them in place.* One down the pecking order, I managed a wristband.

These were our trophies. Partly, I suppose, we grabbed them simply because we could. There was certainly something of the fetish object in many of the finds. What on earth could you usefully do with one of Alan Ball's studs? And, anyway, how would you prove it was his if the International Souvenir and Dressing Room Swag Commission ever called you in to demand authentication? In fact, all I had to go on was its proximity to his peg in the dressing room and a quick look round the boot room to see if anyone else wore aluminium instead of nylon.

It didn't matter. I kept it in my pocket for luck, and later transplanted it to my own left boot, well-Vaselined and with all the torque I could muster on the stud spanner to keep it from coming loose. It was noticeably taller than its nylon companions, and I could feel it through the sole on firmer pitches, spurring me on.

The quality of the available souvenirs increased with our shoe size. Steve was handed down a pair of Colin Harvey's Gola boots, with kangaroo-skin panels on the uppers. I grew into Alan Ball's Hummel. But whatever suppleness they may originally have possessed had evaporated while they'd hung in our garage, and I took a certain pride in rejecting them too.

Sometime after he became first-team coach my father landed the only kit-endorsement deal of his whole career. Stylo paid him a nominal amount to wear their tracksuits and boots. I don't know

what brought the deal about, but I'd like to think his speed had
something to do with it. Everton had a club doctor and physiother-
apist, but in the early '70s it was still the job of the first-team coach
to run onto the pitch, spongebag in hand, to tend to injured players.
My father did it faster than any coach or trainer I have ever seen.
His speed was almost comical, disproportionate – nothing short of
a car crash could justify the urgency with which he launched himself
from the dugout and raced across the field, spilling water as he went,
to administer analgesic spray to an ankle knock. I used to watch
with a mixture of pride and slight embarrassment. In a game that
was already exhibiting major signs of cynicism, it was such a brazen
display of commitment and enthusiasm that it seemed out of place,
a bit of old black-and-white film spliced into the Everton highlights
on *Match of the Day*.

Anyway, the truth was that – jaded as we'd become by the pedigree of our hand-me-downs – we didn't want our father's Stylo
Matchmakers. After the brief side-tying sensation of their launch
on the feet of George Best, they'd become irredeemably naff. Adidas,
Puma, Gola perhaps, if they had some star provenance: these were
the brands that brought you some status on the back field or in the
school team. My older brother, keeper of the family memorabilia,
still has the Stylo Matchmakers in their original box.

The biggest souvenir of the lot we didn't need to go foraging for,
it came to us. In my memory we were playing Cuppies on the back
field when we were interrupted. Proper matches always took a bit
of organisation – knocking on doors to scrape the numbers together,
debating whether the sides were really even, arguing over whose ball
to use. But Cuppies was easy. Half a dozen of us, or however many
there were on a given day, kicking into one goal. It was every man
for himself, with each successive scorer going through until the last
player left in each round was eliminated. In this way the field was

eventually whittled down to two for the final. No need for even numbers to start with, no haggling over who got picked for which side, it was a handy format that could accommodate just about anyone who turned up.

This was a 1970 World Cup edition – Jairzinho, Alan Ball, Francis Lee and Gerd Müller engaged in a perpetual goalmouth scramble – so it must have been late summer, pre- rather than post-season. Not that the game as played on the back field recognised such distinctions. There might have been the odd marathon cricket match in the long school holidays, but for practical purposes our football season had begun when we were old enough to join in and wouldn't pause until puberty. Endless games in a fixture list that stretched further than the ten-year-old eye could see. But this one was interrupted. My mother was calling us in, much too early for tea.

My father's Volkswagen Beetle was parked on the road in front of the house instead of on the drive. He wasn't stopping, something about one of the other coaches having overrun his allotted time leaving us with just a few minutes. Still, he had it with him, tall, antiquely ornate and extremely shiny on the passenger seat: the Football League Championship trophy, which that season belonged to the Everton of West, Wright, Hurst, Labone, Brown, Ball, Harvey, Kendall, Husband, Royle and Morrisey, and for the next quarter of an hour to us.

What could we do with it? A lap of honour up and down the road past the neighbours' front gardens was out of the question – we might drop it. There was really only one option, a team photo. That's what you did with trophies. But there wasn't time to run round to any friends' houses and recruit a full squad. So there were nine of us – seven who'd been battling it out for that afternoon's Jules Rimet trophy, the goalkeeper, and the boy from next door who, strictly speaking, shouldn't have been there. It wasn't that he was a Liverpool fan – two or three of the lads in the picture were – more that he didn't really like football, didn't like us much, and wasn't part of the group that played on the back field. Still, he lived next door, saw his chance and made a late run.

Nine isn't the perfect number for a team picture, especially when three of the nine are equally determined to hold the trophy. The other six were no doubt pretty keen themselves, but having already stumbled into the photo opportunity of their lives to date they weren't going to push their luck. As the oldest by a couple of years, Steve had the strongest claim – as well as the actual strength to enforce it. Mike and I had the presence of our parents to ensure fair play and equality of access.

You can tell from the photo that the solution took a certain amount of choreographing. For my older brother to occupy his rightful captain's position – front row, centre – his two younger siblings would have needed to reach awkwardly across him from either side to register the all-important contact. The compromise relegates him to the back row, allowing us to kneel either side claiming a scrolled handle each, while Steve asserts his seniority by reaching forward to get both hands on the shoulder of the trophy. The object of all the jockeying for proximity stands between us like a portly, silver stork on one leg, unownable.

By the time of the official Everton FC 1970–71 squad photo a few weeks later, the trophy will be reunited with its heavy, plaque-covered wooden base, able to stand unaided in a row of its own at the front; behind it, the Everton players, unlogoed, immaculate. The team picture is the first order of pre-season business, a moment's pause to acknowledge the achievement of last season, before the onslaught of sprints and shuttles and twelve-minute runs designed to sweat them into shape for the new one.

On the front lawn, hastily assembled, our rolling season perpetually at its midway point, we are doing the best we can at short notice. Of the nine of us only one is in full kit. Mike is wearing the

Subbuteo-simple Everton away strip of the early '70s: yellow shirt, blue shorts, yellow socks – four dabs of enamel paint. Three of us on the front row have opted for the one-knee-on-the-ground pose, a couple of decades out of date but at least a stab at professionalism. The effect is spoiled by the other two who are kneeling like choirboys. All of us except one are looking intently at the camera, solemnly pretending that we belong in the picture, or at least that we might grow up to belong in it; that the arrival of the League Championship trophy in Glenmarsh Way was an event that – while not underestimating the strength of the opposition or the challenge ahead of us – we hoped would become a regular occurrence in future seasons. Seasons that would feature us contributing on the field instead of from the complimentary seats.

The one who gives the game away is Puddin'. His real name was Stephen Armstrong and he lived about ten doors down from us towards the main road. Puddin' was so hopeless at football that you'd never willingly pick him for your side, but at the same time he was such an amiable character that no one would ever deny him a game. He usually went in goal. With the rest of us straining for nonchalance, Puddin' has no pretensions to maintain. He knows he's never going to qualify for a repeat of this moment, so why waste it by joining in the po-faced dry run? Instead, he ignores the camera, staring down over my right shoulder at the trophy with a slightly slack-jawed smile. The look on his face is a kind of disbelieving wonder.

Behind us, between the blue floral curtains in the living-room window, you can see a pair of the Lladró figurines Dad used to bring home from foreign tours to make up for the fact that my mother never got to go anywhere. If it wasn't for the reflection of the trees in the garden across the road, you'd be able to see his medal on the wall. The front door has been left open, giving a view down the hall and through the kitchen window towards the back field. In a few moments the League Championship trophy will be in the passenger seat of my father's car heading back to Goodison, and we'll be climbing over the garden fence to resume our dress rehearsal for glory.

As well as being personally liable for Everton's results, our other main responsibility as the sons of our father was to be exceptional players ourselves. At school the expectation that we'd stand out came neatly packaged with a complete lack of credit when we did: *Well, you're bound to be good, because of your dad.* We were good, although of course good was scarcely good enough given our pedigree. Perhaps we expected it too. Football – interest in it, access to it, ability at it – seemed to be a right that came with the surname. It might have been different if one of us had broken ranks and been useless, or grown up hating the game and hiding when the teams were picked. As it was, football was the family business and we each had every intention of eventually following our father into the firm.

He exerted no pressure on us, but when the time came there was a gently delivered professional opinion. My older brother was the first to get it. He went into the printing trade. Mike, four years younger, was a speedy, determined left-back. Not as fast as my father – none of us was, even well into our teens and his forties – but quick and hard and skilful. Everton signed him as an apprentice at sixteen. There was no favouritism: by then my father had been gone from the club for a couple of years. Everton had a surplus of left-backs and Mike could see the line of succession at his position stretching into the distance. But he did well and was made captain of the youth team. It was my father who called the club, close to Mike's eighteenth birthday, to hear that they wouldn't be signing him on as a full professional.

I can remember him walking back in from the hall and I can see Mike wriggling away from him around the far side of the dining-room table, refusing to be consoled, because being consoled meant it was true. My father had probably seen this reaction before from other boys Mike's age, boys who'd gambled on making the grade to the exclusion of making plans for anything else. But he'd never been in the same position himself. His apprenticeship had been as a joiner not a footballer. In the early '50s forging a successful career in the game had been no less of a lottery, but it hadn't yet become a pools win. It certainly wasn't something into which you put your hopes exclusively.

Of course, one club's reject is another club's canny signing, and Mike went on to have a short career with Leeds, Peterborough and Tranmere. He had the guts to retire at the age of twenty-three. He wasn't transfer-listed, or crippled by injury, he simply decided that if he wasn't going to play at the highest level, or couldn't see it happening in the near future, then he'd rather not play at all.

My father accepted the decision, but I don't think he could understand it. An unquenchable passion to play had carried him through cartilage trouble and a slide down the divisions as far as Chelmsford City in the Southern League. Regardless of the opposition or the remuneration, he had played because there was nothing else he'd rather do on any given afternoon than be out on the pitch matching his talent and determination against someone else's. He could always fall back on his skills as a joiner to make a living, and he'd often had to. But it was only his bad knee that finally stopped him playing in benefit matches. How could Mike, fit and strong, the family's best physical specimen, give it up voluntarily?

I secretly admired Mike's decision. I hadn't had what it took to be a professional player. But if I had, I'm not sure I would have had the courage to walk away from it. I played outside-left, my father's position. He told me – and I think I might have preferred it if he hadn't – that I had more ability than he'd had at the same age, which is to say fourteen or so. My problem was my temperament. Everybody knew that, and under the obligation to do justice to my sporting inheritance it got worse.

My father, famously, had never been booked in fourteen seasons as a professional player. The standard package of principles that he drummed into us – play fair, own up, try hard – was one he could back up by his own example. Even the one caution he did eventually pick up, as a coach, was borne out of his fiercely black-and-white view of justice – approaching the referee at the final whistle after an Everton defeat at Derby to harangue him about his failure properly to discharge his duties. My reaction to provocation was usually physical, retaliating against some fourteen-year-old hard-knock with facial hair from Kirkby or Litherland who didn't appreciate a Formby nancy boy beating him for speed or skill.

I can only remember my father coming to watch me play for the school on two occasions, both district cup finals. In the first I hit what seemed then, and still seems now, a miraculous half-volley from barely five yards inside our opponents' half, a distance long enough, in memory, for a slow cross-fade of crowd noise from what-the-hell-is-he-doing to bloody-hell-what-a-goal. It probably had something to do with the height of the opposition keeper between the full-sized posts at Marine FC in Crosby where the final was played, but nonetheless it was a great goal, made greater by the fact that my dad had actually seen it and wouldn't think it an exaggeration in the retelling.

The following year Formby High were back at the same ground in the same final. This time, though, I was apprehensive. Two or three weeks before the game the threats had started: the St Joseph's right-back was going to put me out of the final by breaking my leg. School football on Merseyside always involved a fair bit of physical menace. Traditionally, the best teams came from the toughest areas and Liverpool had plenty of competition. Formby was where Liverpool kids came on day trips to visit the pine woods and the beach; we were too middle class to be allowed to be any good.

Strangely, I knew the boy making the threats. We actually played in the same Sunday league side. But the tribal obligations of school games cut across all other loyalties, and anyway he was a headcase. Early in the game I sealed my own fate by scoring – a free kick which went in and stayed in, lodging behind the stanchion and having to be punched free by an adult.

Then came the promised leg-break attempt. He might as well have produced a baseball bat from down his sock for all the disguise that went into the challenge. He was big and reasonably quick, but he lacked the guile to put the boot in with any finesse. I had pushed the ball past him half expecting it, and when he came in with both feet I jumped high over the danger. All I had to do was land, look aggrieved and hope that the referee would punish the intent rather than the outcome. But while I was up there some overdeveloped sense of injustice took over. Why should he avoid a sending-off simply because I'd had reactions quick enough to save myself from serious injury? Why should it take me being carried off in order for him to get his comeuppance? I landed, turned and swung my left boot as hard as I could in his direction. In coming after me with both feet he had slid in low and was still on the ground. I connected perfectly with his head, just as I had with the free kick. You always know when you've struck it well: there's almost no resistance, just a glorious instant of football physics, a 100-per-cent-efficient transfer of energy from foot to object.

I think I was off the field before I was actually sent off, surrounded by a phalanx of Formby parents and teachers, simultaneously protecting me from the St Joseph's contingent intent on killing me, and resisting the urge to kill me themselves for being so stupid. The St Joseph's right-back was still down as I reached the relative safety of the dressing room, although even inside we could hear the mob banging and shouting threats of retribution through the wooden walls.

I can't remember if my mother spoke, but I know my father did: 'Right, that's you! That's you!' That's you finished is what he meant, but in his fury he didn't have the patience to get to the end of the phrase. I understood him well enough. 'That's you' was like one of my dad's multi-headed screwdrivers; a whole range of sanctions could be fitted on the end of 'That's you'. Worst of all, sometimes none was, leaving you in a limbo of dread about what the punishment might turn out to be.

Not this time. After a minute or two of generalised reproach, sentence was passed. 'If you can't control yourself, then you can't play.' In another context this might have been a coaching homily, impressing on a group of promising youngsters the need for self-expression to be grounded in self-discipline. In the rickety dressing room of Marine FC, with ugly shouts still coming from outside, it was the ultimate punishment – a ban on playing until I could behave myself on the field. Pleading mitigating circumstances was no use with my father. He dealt in certainties, rights and wrongs, and I was clearly wrong. Fizzing with the injustice of it all, I wanted to tell him about the threats, how I was just standing up for myself the way he'd said we should.

It wasn't as if he didn't have a temper of his own. In that respect I was a chip off the old block. But there was no arguing with history; this was the man who'd played 423 league and cup games without ever being booked, let alone sent off in disgrace in a cup final. It was only after he died that my mother told me about Makepeace of Doncaster Rovers.

'Ooh he was a sod, he used to go for your dad every time.'

Brian Makepeace – the name couldn't have been contrived – was a notorious hard man who graduated from the colliery team in Rossington where he was born to Doncaster, where he was captain and right-back for eleven years. He was a year older than my father and had already been in the league for a season when my dad made his debut for Bury, his first professional club. Whenever they met, my father would beat Makepeace and Makepeace would kick my father. That was the basic winger/full-back dynamic, and the level of intimidation had to be fairly high before it would register on the refereeing radar of the '50s. Justice was generally deferred until the perpetrator had the ball himself within range of one of the designated hard men on his victim's team. During one game my father couldn't wait.

'I think it was a night game,' said my mother, 'and he'd clattered Dad a few times and the crowd were getting really worked up. Well, he clattered him again, and your dad had him on the ground, hammering him.'

'What did the ref do?'

'He just said, "Now, now Stewart, I'll deal with this," and they got on with the game. Now of course he would have been sent off.'

'And the ref didn't even book him?'

'Oh no, Dad never got booked, you know that.'

In the end it wasn't my temper that sabotaged my dreams of playing football but something else in my temperament. Or something not sufficiently there. That is to say whatever internal force it was that had propelled my father from a tiny Scottish backwater to the World Cup in Sweden, whatever mechanism it was that hoovered up all the available oxygen around him and turned it into pure effort – whether the game was a cup tie or a charity match.

I had trials with Plymouth Argyle but no offer came, and I drifted off into areas in which I had less to live up to. I may have inherited my father's raw talent, but clearly there'd been more to his success than that. More substantial virtues that he hadn't handed down.

Chapter Two
Leaving Lossiemouth

THE HARBOUR AT LOSSIEMOUTH is full of yachts now, weekend boats that never seem to move, save for the gentle lifting and lowering the tide gives them at their moorings. I'd heard that it had happened, but this was the first time I'd been back to see it for myself.

'It just seems like a waste of a harbour. The east coast of Scotland isn't that suitable for yachting, it's too exposed. On the west coast you can dodge round an island. On the east coast you're either in or you're out, and if you're out at the wrong time, you're out on your own.'

Donnie Stewart, born here like my father in 1932, is Lossiemouth's unofficial historian. In their day – and even in mine on the annual trek north for the family summer holiday – it had been a busy fishing port, the harbour full of trawlers. The town had been built with herring money and maintained by the trade in cod and haddock. The point of the place was emphasised by a gentle camber in the headland on which the whole community was built, the wide handsome streets sloping down to the sea on three sides. The road was for visitors like us coming in from the south. The chief way out for the locals was to the north, east and west, by boat.

I sat in Donnie's living room, a short walk from the water as all Lossie's living rooms are, and listened to him sketch the boundaries of childhood in a fishing community of 5,000.

'We had nothing to do with more than half a mile inland, we'd just no interest in it. I mean we'd go up to Elgin on the bus, but it would never occur to me to get off anywhere in between. That was

country. We were fisher, they were country. You could tell the difference between the town folk and us. They walked different. They
would put their feet down flat whereas here you walked on your
toes because fishermen were used to balancing. So you could literally tell the difference as they walked down the street. England? I
don't think we ever thought of England really.'

Why bother? Once past the massive stone bulwarks at the mouth
of the harbour there was the whole ocean-going world to choose
from. And since every man set out to sea knowing there was a good
chance he might not return, a fair number of them decided to make
one-way journeys of their own choosing: Canada, America, Australia,
New Zealand. The masthead of the local paper bore the legend: *The
Northern Scot, A Popular Journal For Scotsmen At Home And Abroad.*
There was a weekly 'Kith and Kin' feature with photos of those
who'd made it safely across.

Alexander Davidson, who went to Canada 21 years ago, is a
groom on a farm in Nanton near Calgary.

John Reid, born Lossiemouth, February 1866, has died at his
home, 4057 N. Interstate, Portland, Oregon.

Those seemed to be the options on offer to the men of
Lossiemouth: leave and never come back, or stay and perhaps never
come back anyway. In either case, the people of the town faced
largely out to sea and not back over their shoulders.

The exceptions were my father and Ramsay MacDonald. Growing
up it had seemed to me like a handy pairing: Lossiemouth's two
most notable sons, the footballer and the politician, heading south
to make their names along the road we drove in on every year. By
the time my father had reached the age of five, Ramsay MacDonald
was already back – in the cemetery up at Spynie, bedded in for the

long wait for history to rehabilitate him. Some of the local children sat on their parents' shoulders to watch the funeral cortège pass by, but I can't imagine my grandfather allowing himself the luxury of time off work.

John Imlach was a man of the utmost correctness in all areas of his life. The town relied on it – he was the regional superintendent for the Scottish Boatowners Mutual Insurance Association. A marine engineer, he'd been to sea himself, only leaving the merchant navy to spend more time at home when my father was born. On land he was respected, and occasionally feared, for his fairness. If he said a boat needed repairing there was no disputing it. If a ship sank, he would travel to the courtrooms in Edinburgh to give his opinion as to whether or not it had been done deliberately.

He had absolutely no interest in football. If he had, it would certainly have been documented. John Imlach maintained records of everyday life as though they too might later be called into evidence. In notebooks he kept the details of every car he ever owned, recording the purchase price, the sale price and the particulars and cost of any repair work. Ancillary tables charted the rising price of petrol through the years. When he was ill he made case notes, hour-by-hour, and presented them to the doctor on his arrival at the house. His own death he oversaw with punctilious dignity, refusing to leave his home and go to hospital for any kind of treatment that might prolong his life: 'I'm a car that's run and done.'

Having ordered his affairs, and with most of his extended family either under the same roof or within a two-mile radius, his English grandchildren became the last outstanding order of business. My father made the journey home every year of his life, regular as a salmon. But after fifteen years of family holidays in Lossiemouth, we'd all grown up, started careers, travelled abroad and – one way or another – failed to get back there each summer. There was no formal request but, feeling that it was about time, the three of us organised a trip. His Mini (purchase price recorded, sale details pending) had stood, undriven by him, outside the house for months. He managed to get out of his room for a day trip with us. We visited as many of the fishing ports under his old jurisdiction as we could – Buckie, Findochty, Portsoy – and he was recognised and well received on the harbour-sides in all of them. Three weeks after the holiday we were back in Lossiemouth for the funeral. Once we'd left, he'd taken to his bed with the quiet satisfaction of a man who'd finished a large filing job that had been preying on his mind.

My father came from a male line of alternating Johns and Jameses, so if there was any debate at all in advance of his christening it can only have been over the minor placings. Names in Lossiemouth weren't subject to fashion, they were given in the literal sense – handed on from a current or past owner as a badge of family continuity. That was part of it, I suppose, especially with the frightening annual turnover of names at sea. It was also, perhaps, an expression of natural thrift. Why spoil a child with a new name when there were perfectly good ones in the house that could be reused?

Of course, having given the new arrival a name identical to that of half his relatives and a third of the rest of the town, his family then had to give him another in order to avoid confusion. The phone book is the last place you'll find anyone in Lossiemouth – the streets are awash with nicknames, sea-names, mother's maiden names, and every conceivable alternative to the information originally handed over to the registrar.

My dad got both barrels – he was christened James John – and for individuality's sake had to revert to the third name on his birth certificate. Apart from official envelopes addressed to J.J.S. Imlach Esq., which always looked stylish on the doormat as well as slightly menacing, he'd never been known as anything other than Stewart, until he got ill. It used to upset my mother on visits to the hospital to find that a fresh shift of nurses, with nothing to go on but the information on his chart, had printed James on the card above his bed. It was bad enough that he was slipping away from her, without his name preceding him. He couldn't see the card and that made it worse, as though he were the unwitting victim of an office joke, tottering towards the exit with a kick-me sign on his back. One more indignity to add to the long list that illness had brought with it. But, without realising, the nurses were perhaps putting him in his proper place, reconnecting him to the long family file of Jameses and Johns dot-dashing their way back down the Imlach line.

My father had discovered at the age of fifteen that he'd be the first Imlach in five generations not to take the family name to sea. That is, he took it to sea once and brought it home in a sick bag. The custom was for a boy to make his trial voyage on the trawlers as the ship's cook, packed off with a parcel of food already prepared by his mother to minimise the damage he might do to crew morale. My father went out on *The Snowdrop*, the boat of his Grandad Dovey, and was sick enough that he had to be tied to the wheelhouse so that the men could get some fishing done. It was, perhaps, the pivotal episode of his life. Until then my father may have dreamed of being a footballer, but he'd assumed that he would go to sea, where trips to the fishing grounds would blow holes in the fixture list and the game would become a weekend passion. Exhausted and queasy as the boat returned to harbour, he realised only that he had to find a way to make a living on land; he must have felt that his horizons had shrunk not broadened. He rode the butcher's delivery bike for a year until he was old enough to start an apprenticeship as a joiner. Football may have been his life, but there was nothing in the history of the family, or the community, to suggest that it could ever be a livelihood.

What leap of imagination had it taken to change that? My love of football had been handed to me ready-made, it was in my blood.

But it hadn't been in his. He was an only son, with two sisters, and a father who never played the game and seldom willingly watched it. Perhaps its endless improvisation offended my grandfather's sense of order. Once, after his son had turned professional, he was cajoled down to England to see him play. On the Richter scale of local sports journalism this registered as a newsworthy event, and he had a visit from a reporter on his return. What had he thought? 'Och, I've seen games just as good on the square round the corner from my house.'

The square is still round the corner, but now from the house of my dad's sister, May, and her husband Slater, who had better sea legs than my father and did forty years on the trawlers when the fishing was still good. It doesn't look that promising as a football pitch. It's large enough, but the grass playing surface is divided by diagonal footpaths into a St Andrew's flag of four awkward triangles. Either the games they played were extremely narrow affairs, or the wingers on one flank would suddenly find themselves negotiating a strip of concrete as they headed towards the byline to get a cross in. My father and his friends would play football anywhere, but this was the focal point of the endless impromptu kickabout that his childhood telescopes down to in the memories of those who lived it with him. By the time he was a teenager, the games on the square were so popular that large crowds were regularly gathering to watch them. In May 1948 the town council's Playground and Recreation Committee recommended a ban.

He was growing up in a period that saw football in general becoming massively more popular than it had been before or has been since. Attendances at Football League games reached their peak in the '40s. But in Lossiemouth all there was to do was play. The covered market was the closest they had to an indoor pitch if the weather was bad; hosed down after the fish had all been auctioned off, but narrow and with a slope towards one end, where there was the constant danger of the ball going into the harbour and having to be fished out with a loop of rope.

Football matches in the fish market were merely against harbour regulations. On Sundays, when even the swings in the playground were locked up to preserve the fierce peace of the Presbyterian Sabbath, they were against the express wishes of God. With golf prohibited too, the kickabout moved on to the fairways of the relief course after church. There was no dodging the ultimate spectator, but at least their elders were less likely to see them out on the links.

'My earliest memory of your father – we lived at the top of the square and he lived at the bottom – was him crossing the square to school, and he always had a ball, a small ball, at his feet.' Joe Campbell, five years my father's senior, was measuring out the whisky and water – 'I ration myself with this stuff, but not tonight, not tonight' – and settling in to supply me with information. I was doing the rounds of Lossiemouth's sitting rooms, some of which used to be obligatory items on the holiday agenda when I was a child. Unavoidable periods of detention between us and the beach.

Our exact connections to some of our blood relatives were difficult enough to grasp on these once-a-year visits (*'You know Auntie Katie, well, she's Dad's auntie really, now her brother . . .'*); anyone outside the family was usually just another set of kindly faces proffering plates of cakes. The generations were difficult to sort out too. My father was tanned from training and playing outside, yet it was hard to believe he'd been in the same class at school with some of the leathered, salt-cured faces that loomed over us. But although we couldn't always tell who was who, it was clear to us as children that we were important members of this network of cheerful, heavily accented people, and it made no difference to them how long it had been since our last visit. We could walk the streets on the first day of our holiday, without my father, and be recognised as Imlachs by half a dozen passers-by in succession. There was a powerful force at work here that had nothing to do with football.

Our annual return was celebrated in Lossiemouth not because my father was the local hero, but simply because he was local. Leaving Lossie was common; coming back a rarity. I sat with May and Slater one evening during my trip, watching an old video of the annual fishermen's outing: 'He's away . . . aye, Joe, he's away . . . he's away, an a' . . . they're all away, those boys.' The threat from the sea had receded greatly with the end of the fishing industry, but departure and death – synonymous everywhere – were still pointedly so here.

Now I was back for the first time in fifteen years, sipping whisky and underlining my ignorance. Every question sounded like a guilty plea to the sin of omission on my part: *I should know this stuff*. And every casual aside '. . . aye well, as I'm sure he'll have told you himself . . .' came at me like an accusation: *You should know this stuff*. I criss-crossed the town on foot, making door-to-door enquiries: Donnie Stewart; Joe Campbell, who had helped run the St James' youth club team; Johnny Archibald, my father's coach at Lossie juniors and older brother of his teammate Eddie; Colin Tough, his earliest childhood playmate; Robbie Campbell, who was back on holiday having left to play professionally himself; Sandy Reid, who could have done the same but decided to stay.

They all confided their various truths, which intersected at awkward angles with each other, or ran parallel, rival realities which couldn't both have happened. Some were easy to sift out: the goal he scored for Lossiemouth when the dates show he'd long since turned professional. Others I was reluctant to check on, out of respect for the vehemence of the source, or the sheer pleasure shared between storyteller and listener. These men's versions of my father, with their time-slips and game-shifts, were just as valid as the match reports in the *Northern Scot*.

Laying out all the accounts, one on top of another, the young

Stewart started to emerge from the shaded areas – a sort of Venn diagram of his early days and the intensity with which he willed himself beyond the confines of what was locally possible.

'He practised,' Donnie Stewart told me. 'We played, he practised. If it was "three and in" he didn't want to go in goal, so if he scored three maybe I'd go in goal. I was there to enjoy myself, he was concentrating, always trying to improve himself, dribbling a ball up to school and back to improve his control.'

But who was he copying? The nearest professional team was seventy miles away in Aberdeen. Following football would have been more of an effort than playing it, and almost entirely a work of the imagination. There was radio commentary, but only for special fixtures like Scotland–England internationals. My father and his friends would sit round the wireless at home or in the back of Dominic's Café, each supplying their own visuals to go with Raymond Glendenning's plummy English commentary. Occasionally, newsreel highlights of big games would be shown before the main feature at the Regal Cinema in the square – the FA Cup Final, the Scottish Cup Final, Moscow Dynamo against Rangers on their 1945 tour of Britain. But they were exceptions. In the main, football was a game you saw in person or not at all.

My father's favourite player was George Hamilton – Gentleman George – Aberdeen's cultured inside-right. But in order to idolise Hamilton, he first had to assemble him: watching for the Aberdeen results in the paper; scouring the match reports for telling detail of how Hamilton had beaten this man, or laid on that goal; cutting out the rare pictures. This was the raw material out of which he fashioned a professional game to follow and a hero to model himself on.

Eventually, George Hamilton and the Aberdeen centre-half, Frank Dunlop, were booked into the Drill Hall in Elgin, the nearest town of any size, for a 'Demonstration of Soccer Skills'. These tours were one of the few ways professionals could supplement their weekly wages. All the local boys were there, hypnotised by sheer proximity as Hamilton and Dunlop went through their routine: keeping the ball up, heading, passing, giving tips on tactics and training. But it was my father asking all the questions at the end, and taking the answers to heart. Work hard during the week, said Gentleman George, and Saturdays will be easy, and so he was out on the beach in the evenings running himself into the ground.

George Hamilton's visit to the Elgin Drill Hall would have remained the highlight of my father's football education had it not been for the Second World War.

In the '30s two foreign institutions had come to the outskirts of Lossiemouth: the RAF and Gordonstoun. The latter was known locally as the German school after its founder Kurt Hahn, who'd smartly sidestepped the Nazis to pursue his dream of offering robust education for young men in the bracing setting of the Moray Firth. The future Duke of Edinburgh, yet to be groomed for the job of shaking hands and insulting minorities, was just another young aristocrat who'd been sent up to Scotland to have his character built. 'I don't think any of us had any great interest or animosity towards Gordonstoun,' Donnie Stewart told me. 'They were just strange people wanting to wear shorts and sleep in uncomfortable beds. We slept in uncomfortable beds, but we didn't pay to do it.'

The airforce base was a different matter, a focus of fascinated interest for the local children. It was from RAF Lossiemouth that the Lancasters of 617 Squadron, the Dambusters, took off for Norway carrying the Tallboy bombs that would sink the Tirpitz. It was the reason for the concrete blocks on the West Beach, lines of crude sandcastles from square buckets stretching out into the sea to defend against enemy landing craft. One day, a small group of boys stood by the shoreline and watched as the wing sheared off a Wellington shortly after take-off. The wing landed on one of the fairways of the links course by the West Beach; the plane ditched onto the rocks and the crew was killed. My father and his friends spent the week liberating ammunition from the wreckage, dismantling the bullets and using the cordite to light fires on the sand.

Another Wellington went down in a fir plantation during a training run. The pilot and the bomb-aimer both died and the navigator lost a leg, but the wireless operator was lucky. Stan Mortensen, not yet of Blackpool and England, walked away from the wreckage with only a head injury that needed a dozen stitches. Local folklore sometimes conflates the two crashes into a single story which features Mortensen, at the controls of his own plane, executing an emergency landing on the golf course and finishing up in one of the bunkers.

It's true that Stan Mortensen was in Lossiemouth, though, and he wasn't alone. He had teammates in the army base not far away at Pinefield. In fact, the Second World War was responsible for producing a string of impossible football teams; teams that could only otherwise have existed in pub arguments and best-of lists. The cream of the English and Scottish leagues were in the services, and turned out as guest players for whichever local team got in first to claim them. The RAF played the Army, the British Services played the Scottish Services, an Aberdeen select eleven made up of Arsenal, Everton, Third Lanark and Raith Rovers men played anybody who could muster a side to take them on.

It was like a vision of the future. Years before threatened players' strikes, Bosman and European Court rulings, the war had blown a hole in the Football League's restrictive transfer system. For a surreal and – in footballing terms – sublime few years, some of the best players in the country were effectively hanging around Highland League grounds, boots in hand, hopping from one foot to another in the hope of getting a game.

Until Lossiemouth were admitted to the Highland League in 1946 – a cheer rang out one night at the Regal when the news was flashed up on the screen – the only organised football my father would have been able to watch was five miles away at Elgin. The nets at Borough Briggs were as much of a draw as the action on the field. He and his friends would take a ball of their own and kick into the back of one goal while the play was up the other end.

But the war meant that suddenly he was offered the chance to see newsreel-quality football at radio-commentary length. Stan Mortensen turned out in Elgin colours against a series of forces select teams. In June 1943 the Morayshire Services played Aberdeenshire Services, giving him a close-up look at home-grown heroes like Eddie Turnbull, Willie Woodburn and Bobby Brown. The following year brought a proxy international – a British Army XI against the Scottish Services. Large gatherings were prohibited except in special circumstances, but security considerations were overridden by the need for fundraising. Warship Week in August 1944 meant that people could crowd into Borough Briggs with a clear conscience, knowing that their ninepence would be going towards buying a new frigate. Joe Mercer of Everton and England led the British Army. His ex-teammate Dixie Dean was up front for the Scottish Services.

The line-up for the Victory in Europe match nine months later was even better. Stan Mortensen and Stanley Matthews – their careers yet to coincide at Blackpool – took the field together for the RAF against a Morayshire services team. The services had England's Bert Williams in goal, Carlisle's Bill Shankly, Frank Soo of Leicester, Charlton's Harold Hobbs. Alongside Matthews and Mortensen were Stoke and England's Neil Franklin and Leslie Smith of Aston Villa. More than 5,000 paid the shilling to get in, among them my thirteen-year-old father, in the queue early to make sure of a spot at the front where he could see.

These fixtures were packed with people from his future: Eddie Turnbull would be a teammate at the 1958 World Cup; Stanley Matthews a regular opponent in the 1st Division; in 1959 he would play Joe Mercer's Aston Villa side in the semi-final of the FA Cup; later Bill Shankly, who could virtually climb over the wall of his back garden into Everton's training ground, would sit with him drinking tea and trading grizzled wisdom in the afternoons at Bellefield, when the players had left.

Could this game have been the occasion that created the first chink in the outer wall of his ambition? This wasn't a newsreel, it was an international fixture within a bus ride of his house, an actual game with the actual Stanley Matthews kicking into the goals he regularly played behind. If these players could come to where he lived, then maybe the return journey was possible.

On my rounds I was carrying with me a couple of team photographs, the only football pictures I had of my father in his Lossiemouth days. I had no idea which team it was, but everybody I met knew straight away. 'Oh, that's the Rob Roys. Good God, look at the size of him!'

My father was never very big – the tallest any of his professional clubs dared to list him at was 5'6" – but in these pictures he looks ridiculous. Tiny, skinny, he's more like the mascot than the team's best player, the annoying nipper who keeps sneaking into the shot alongside his Brylcreemed elders and betters.

The Rob Roys, it turned out, were a short-lived team formed to play in the Elgin Summer League of 1947, which, on the evidence of the picture, they'd won. The captain is being held rather uncertainly aloft by his teammates and in the space beneath him two young lads, their discarded bike just visible off to the right, are lying on the ground to get into the picture. My father, the top of his head comfortably cleared by the chin of the player behind him, looks like he belongs back there with them. The shoulder seam of his jersey is halfway towards his elbow and there's little evidence of any underlying structure for the elastic of his shorts to hold on to. The date of the picture would make him fifteen – although he looks a lot younger – while the rest of the team are clearly young men.

'Oh aye, they're all two, three, four years older than your dad, fishermen, apprentices at Sutherlands engineering and that. But he was centre-forward, you know.'

I had known this, that he'd started off at centre-forward, but looking at this picture it made no sense. The Rob Roys, one-season wonders that they were, had survived down the years thanks to a local photographer who must have been on hand for their final game. I'd been hoping that the picture was of the St James' youth club team, a group of boys who had played their way into local legend.

As well as my father there had been Robbie Campbell, an elegant centre-half who went on to play for Hearts and Cowdenbeath, and Eddie Archibald, who was an outside-right and signed for St Mirren. Sadly, the key witness to the birth of this team was dead. Everyone I went to see had plenty to tell me, but the conversations all began the same way. 'The guy who could have told you stories galore just died last year – Joe Edwards. Joe was outstanding, a great fella, it was him that got all these boys together as a team.'

It was the start of a pattern that seemed designed to underline to me how late I'd left the whole enterprise. His first mentor at Lossiemouth, his closest friend and best man at Bury, his best mate and roommate at Nottingham Forest; they'd all outlived my father, but not by long enough to tell me anything about him.

Joe Edwards had been a useful Highland League player himself, but his knees gave out when he was still in his early twenties, so he decided to coach. Until then, football for players of my father's age had been one long formless kickabout. Up to school, on the square, along the wide traffic-less streets, across the golf course, through the fish market, a fabulous free-for-all. Joe Edwards brought some order to it, with the help of Joe Campbell who was club secretary.

According to the surviving Joe, his friend had made the change that effectively created my father's career: 'It was Joe Edwards who turned your father into a left-winger, because he was right-footed. It was Joe who saw it as a weakness that he couldn't kick with his left and put him on the left wing. Left-wingers were rare – like butter y'know, they were a rationed item.' From other people's accounts it was less clear-cut; my father had decided on his own to start cultivating his weaker foot, setting himself the task of dribbling to school and back every day without using his right. The basic facts, though, weren't in dispute, except with my childhood certainties.

I'd grown up knowing that there were key characteristics I'd inherited from my father: his height, his speed, his passion for football – and his position on the field. It was a source of pride that we both wore number 11, and that we were left-footed, valuable commodities in an overwhelmingly right-sided game. I suppose a little reflection would have yielded up the insight that I must have exercised some choice, consciously or not, in opting to play my dad's position. But being left-footed was just something that had been passed down in the genes, no choice about that. Mike kicked with his left too; it was Steve who was in the minority out on the right.

But left-footedness, it turned out, was something my father had simply willed into existence, along with the family football tradition. More than that, he'd done it so successfully, ingrained it so deeply, that somehow it had lodged in his DNA and become an inheritable trait, created from nothing, and passed on to his children.

His friend Sandy Reid was a naturally left-sided player. He welcomed me at his front door – the same height as my father, but with the fair complexion suggested by his name – and led me through into the living room on stiff joints, rocking slightly as he favoured one side. The act of sitting down was skilfully executed, but clearly something he needed to brace himself for.

'Noo then, fit d'ye want to ken aboot?'

He sounded like my father would have if he'd never left Lossiemouth. The way he used to sound on Sunday phone calls home to May, standing in the hall growing progressively more Scottish, while we sat in the living room listening and laughing. Sandy was the player that got away, or more accurately, the one that never got away. With his dog asleep beside him on the sofa and his wife in the armchair opposite, nodding and smiling, I was looking at my father in a parallel life, the one in which he said no to a trial with an English club. The best team Sandy ever played for remains his first.

'A'body kent what y'was gan t'dae. Robbie was centre-half and I was inside-left. I never used to look for the ba' – when the ba' came up and Robbie was going to head it, I just moved o'er and he just always nodded it over to the left . . . always. Y'kent ain another – even mair so than some of them big teams nowadays – y'kent what was going to happen. It's never been the same since, I don't think, nae in my head anyway. Nah, nae as good.'

'They say you might have been the best of the lot, Sandy.'

'I don't know, that's what they say but . . . I was a fool for m'self really.'

Sandy's football career, like most at the time, was interrupted by National Service. (My father had a perforated eardrum, to Bury's later relief.) It didn't have to be much of an interruption, though. Good players quickly became regimental favourites, and Sandy settled in as wireless operator and star inside-left for the Royal Artillery at Andover. 'Oor battery sergeant-major was a scout and after two or three games he says to me, "Right, you're going on a two-week trial to Everton." I said, "Ach, I'm nae going." I didna' go – stupid eh?'

'Why not?'

'I don't know, I just didna' go. I wished I'd went, y'ken – nothing to lose. I still played for the regiment, like, till I was demobbed. I aye look at Everton right up to noo on the TV to see how they're daein', ken? Mebbe I'd a' met Stewart if I'd gotten into that after I was demobbed, like . . . ach I dinna ken if I'd have made the grade or no . . .'

While he was stationed at Andover Sandy did meet up with my father and Robbie Campbell, to see Scotland play England at Wembley. It was 1955 and my father had just joined Nottingham Forest. Within three years he'd be playing for Scotland himself. Sandy went back and played for Lossiemouth.

'Aye, very first game back for Lossie, up at Fort George against the Army. Early in the game I went up to head the ba', the keeper came oot, put up his knee and broke my arm. They said they heard the crack right roon' the pitch. So that was me in the hospital Saturday night. You got no pity on a Saturday night, they thought everyone was drunk. So they just bandaged it – it was swinging aboot like this. Oh it was sair the weekend. I had to go back and have it done again, they'd done it wrong. I never forgot that – the things that stick, eh?'

It's a phrase he uses more than once. Lots of things have stuck with Sandy, perhaps because nothing's come along since to dislodge them, details that I'm sure would have been long lost to my father if ever I'd sat down with him like this. He'd have been more like Robbie Campbell – happy to talk, but short on specifics. Robbie didn't manage quite the career my father did despite his ability. Still, he had four seasons with Hearts to remember, a move to Cowdenbeath and 150 professional games before he left to join the police force.

The games and goals still shiny in Sandy Reid's mind had been crowded out in Robbie's and my father's, pennies in an arcade game pushed over the edge by the steady supply of new ones. At St James' youth club, though, they'd all been together, stacking up the future anecdotes a game at a time. Hat-tricks, late-game heroics, endless wins against older teams from bigger towns. In 1949 St James' record read: Played 44, Won 44, Goals for 104, Goals against 4. Even an all-star eleven made up of the best players from every other team in the league couldn't beat them.

I finally came across a picture of that team; someone had found it in a drawer and sent it in to the local paper. Sandy Reid and my father are sitting next to each other on the end of the front row. Sandy may be slightly stockier, but there's nothing to choose between them: arms folded, ankles crossed, hair slicked back. They played together, dived from the harbour wall in summer, teamed up for cycling holidays. From May to October they all lived together in tents up by the lighthouse beyond the West Beach, cooking their meals outdoors. It was a Lossiemouth tradition, a rehearsal for leaving home.

When it came time to graduate from St James' to the Lossie juniors team – one level below the Highland League – they'd all gone together. But then, piece by piece, the tight group that Joe Edwards had moulded started to fragment. Robbie Campbell signed for Lossiemouth's Highland League side, followed by my father. A couple of the older lads got their call-up papers.

The Highland League was the pinnacle of local footballing achievement, which is to say that it was the highest anyone had ever gone. But a local scout had been watching the St James' generation from the beginning. Willie Shanks was a referee from Elgin, who'd offici-ated at some of their early matches, and had connections with a number of English clubs, Second Division Bury among them. Robbie Campbell was the first to head south to try his luck. In November 1951 the *Northern Scot* sent him on his way with a back-page edito-rial: 'When you leave next Monday you will be carrying the wishes of every North soccer fan.' Robbie carried them back again a few weeks later, having decided that a landlocked mill town wasn't somewhere he'd like to settle.

My father was next to try, the following Easter. He travelled down to Bury on the eve of Good Friday 1952 and immediately played three games over the holiday weekend, scoring on his debut. Before the month was up he'd signed. A week later, the *Northern Scot* reported that Eddie Archibald had gone to Portsmouth on trial. Lossiemouth had never produced a professional footballer before and hasn't since. Joe Edwards's church youth team turned out three. Three and an asterisk.

Before I left Sandy Reid's house for the short walk back to May's where I was staying, he rolled up his trouser leg to show me the cause of his stilted gait – a long scar arching ungracefully around his knee joint. It was a double of the one my father had, the mark of a cartilage operation in the days before keyhole surgery.

'That's nae the fitba'. Years as a slater – that's why that's gone. Up on roofs a' my days in snow and a'thing. Wear and tear . . . wear and tear, that's what I put it down to. Look, it'll nae bend. Strong enough but it'll nae bend.'

Chapter Three

Retain-and-transfer:
Bury 1952–54

S HORTLY AFTER THE RESIDENTS of Colindale board the Northern
Line for their morning commute south into central London,
two groups of people set off the other way, into the past.

Turn left out of the tube station for the RAF Museum (don't
forget the Airfix shop on the way back), turn right and cross the
road for the British Newspaper Library. We had scrapbooks full of
cuttings at home, but they were all highlights and headlines, sort
of a director's cut of my father's career. Here's where the rushes
were stored.

Eventually the millions of pages of newsprint stacked decades-
deep in this utilitarian brick Tardis will be kept nowhere. All of it
will be on an unlocatable series of hard drives that anyone can access
from their computer, sitting at home or in a café: all the exclusives,
the obits, the declarations of war and denials of adultery scanned
in and searchable by keywords or dates. It will be a massive conven-
ience and a great pity.

For the moment though, The Past, Contemporaneous Reports Of,
has a geographical presence, two stops from the end of the Edgware
Branch; you can visit it. I wasn't expecting to make up for the years
of unasked questions in here – I didn't have that much faith in journalism. I was looking for the kind of material my father wouldn't
have been able to supply anyway, a solid framework, not just of dates
and games and goals, but also injuries, off-days, missed sitters and
rows with the boss.

The story began in weekly instalments every Saturday in the

Northern Scot. When he turned professional it became twice-weekly, the Bury *Times* offering a Wednesday as well as a weekend episode. By the time he reached Nottingham his career had gone daily, with a double helping on Saturdays when the *Evening Post* would give a cliffhanging account of Forest's first twenty minutes and the *Football Post* would finish off the storyline with the result and a full account of the game a couple of hours later.

I sat and rooted futilely for him in retrospect. I hadn't expected this, to be gripped by a narrative I couldn't influence and whose outcome in any case I knew perfectly well. Yet I celebrated when he broke through into the first team, cheered his goals and wished injury, or a poor performance at the very least, on anyone who took his place when he was dropped or out hurt. I transcribed match reports with a kind of press-box urgency, as though I were channelling a real-time account of the game: '*A splendid equaliser came in the 13th minute. Plant broke through on the right and when he pulled the centre back Imlach, who had moved into the middle, volleyed it with tremendous speed past the hapless Hardwick*.'

I could hear the portable typewriters, and the reporters reading their pieces over the phone to the copy-takers. I'd done the same myself at Anfield and Goodison Park: 'Imlach, that's I-M-L-A-C-H, who had moved into the middle . . .'

Perhaps it was the straight-faced innocence of the language that drew me in, the days of Splendid Equalisers and Hapless Hardwicks. I came across a claim from an irate losing manager: 'We were robbed.' Another piece started with a post-match quote from Doncaster Rovers' boss, the former Irish international Peter Doherty: 'It's a funny game is football.' Good God, surely I hadn't stumbled on its first recorded usage? At the very least, these had to be early sightings, portraits of the cliché as a young quote, before repetition had made it meaningless, then humorous and, finally, archly postmodern. I was reading football-manager in the original.

My dad's career kicked off on microfilm. To save its fragile fibres the *Northern Scot* had been preserved on the futuristic format of yesteryear. The microfilm viewing room at the British Newspaper Library is a serious and silent place – save for the squeaky spooling of the machines – where illumination of all kinds is strictly rationed. At any one time each customer is allowed no more than four items from the archive and a small splash of light – enough to see, but not so much as to overlap onto anyone else's. People guard their lit patches of the past like cave dwellers, suspicious of passers-by who might be angling for a historical insight over their shoulder.

I was glad to get into the light when he turned pro. In the main reading rooms the bound volumes of newspapers are delivered on ancient trolleys by whispering porters. They have to be propped up on large wooden lecterns that reproduce the classic five-past-one reading angle at which you might hold the paper yourself if it wasn't attached to twenty-five other editions and weighed the best part of thirty pounds. The pages have to be peeled gently in slow motion – too much wrist and the tear can be heard around the room. But even handled carefully the heavy volumes lose weight on every trip out of the vaults. The past is as much inhaled here as it is read. And when the bell sounds at the end of the afternoon, each reading place has its own crumbly covering of newsprint filings to show for the day's foraging.

Long after he'd left Lossiemouth for the English Second Division, the *Northern Scot* had kept running regular stories on my father, reporting back to Scotsmen at home on yet another who had gone abroad. In the Bury *Times'* 1952–53 season preview, though, he didn't rate a mention. Unsurprising really, since he started as a part-timer in the fourth team.

The minutes of Bury's board meeting for May 1952 show that they paid Lossiemouth a transfer fee of £150. Later, the Highland

League team must have felt they'd struck a poor bargain. The minutes from January the following year record that: 'A letter was read from Lossiemouth AFC regarding the signing of Stewart Imlach and it was agreed to send a further donation of £50.' My father was to receive £6 a week during the summer and £7 during the season, rising to £14, which was the league maximum, if he was in the first team.

He was twenty when he signed for Bury and still had nine months of his joinery apprenticeship left; giving up a solid trade for the short-lived, long-odds life of a professional footballer would have been against everything his parents believed in. The club found a local joinery firm where he could finish serving his time, and digs with a landlady who already had a couple of other young players in the house. There was nothing exceptional in his situation. At the start of the '52–53 season Bury had a playing staff of thirty-two, which included one amateur, four servicemen, and eight part-timers including my father.

Over the first few weeks of that season I watched him surface through the back-page newsprint at startling speed. On 20 August he was listed as a scorer for the B team against the A. The following week he was promoted to the A team line-up. Seven days later, on 3 September, he moved into the reserves and scored in a 3–0 win. On 10 September the reserves won again, while the first team lost. In fact, the first team was without a win in its opening half-dozen games. On Wednesday 17 September the Bury *Times* back-page headline read: 'YOUNG FORWARDS IN TEAM TO MEET PLYMOUTH.' There were three of them: my father, his roommate in digs, Eddie Gleadall, who'd actually made his senior debut the previous season, and Bobby Dale. The climb from fourth string to first team had taken him a playing month. He had to be called down off the roof of a house he was working on to be given the news.

Away at Plymouth the revamped Bury line-up managed a 0–0 draw to pick up what was only their third point of the season. In their next game they won at Southampton. The local paper scrambled to feature the three newcomers before their home debut the following week.

Their pictures are stripped down an inside page: Gleadall in action, Dale during a training session. My father is at his workbench in overalls and a cloth cap, self-consciously sawing a piece of two-by-four for the camera. Since his job meant that he could train only on Tuesday and Thursday nights, he'd been at work when the pre-season photo call took place, and the paper had evidently had to send out a photographer to get whatever picture he could for the story. It looks a little strange on the sports page, and faintly ludicrous next to its neighbours as one in a series of three rising stars, but it locates him as a footballer of his time as well as any endorsement shot of David Beckham's. Football was a game of the working class, for the working class, by the working class. One thing it wasn't was a golden passport out of the working class.

In significant ways footballers were actually worse off than the crowds watching them from the terraces on a Saturday afternoon. True, their standard working day – two or three hours of physical exercise – was usually over by lunchtime, and they had the potential, at least, to earn more than most labourers. In 1952 the average manual wage in the UK was £8 13s. Footballers could earn up to £14 during the season and £10 during the summer – if they were on the league maximum. According to Players' Union figures, though, only 20 per cent of them were. As late as 1955, the union put the average footballer's wage at £8, by which time factory workers were earning closer to £11.

No other industry in the country had a maximum wage. Football clubs were alone in operating a cartel that imposed an arbitrary ceiling on the earnings of their employees. And the minimum retaining wage they were obliged to pay a player was £322 a year, a little over £6 a week. That innocent-sounding term 'retaining wage' was the pointer to a more fundamental problem. The real disadvantage footballers saw when they compared themselves to the ranks of working men who paid to watch them every week was their lack of freedom. The lads from the feltworks and the cotton mill and Benson's toffee factory may have had tough, unrewarding jobs, but at least they were free to leave one for another.

My father's apprenticeship as a joiner lasted five years, from the age of sixteen until his twenty-first birthday. The contract he signed with Bury FC gave the club the rights to his services in perpetuity. Not that he enjoyed a reciprocal commitment from them. His contract – every footballer's contract – was for twelve months only. At the end of a season clubs could release a player, put him up for sale, or retain him – often on reduced wages if the team had a bad year. Any player who refused to agree terms, whatever they might be, would be paid no wages. Not paid no wages and sacked, or released, but paid no wages and retained. If he walked out he couldn't play anywhere else because the club held his registration. If he demanded a transfer they could simply refuse – or put a price on his head so high that it was a refusal by other means.

And while he was on the transfer list they weren't obliged to pay him. A man sitting at home with an artificially high market value and no income had limited options. The majority caved in. Those whose principles wouldn't let them had no choice but to leave the professional game altogether. Three years before my father joined Bury, T.G. Jones, the great centre-half and captain of Wales, had caused an uproar when he walked out on Everton for non-league Pwllheli FC. It had been his only means of escape from a club that had him on the transfer list but refused to sell him.

John McNeil, the manager who signed my father for Bury, had cut the players' wages on his arrival at the club two seasons earlier. The team's right-back at the time was Cyril Fairclough, the first professional full-back my dad ever lined up against, in his trial game.

Cyril was a solid, one-club man who spent twelve seasons with Bury, before playing and managing non-league. He'd scouted until he was seventy-eight, and was proud of having watched more than seventy games in his final season on the road for Manchester United.

I sat talking to his wife while he tried and failed to find some paperwork he wanted to show me. They'd sold their family house to buy a retirement flat overlooking the cricket ground in Urmston – closer to Old Trafford than Bury's Gigg Lane – and his playing career was temporarily lost to him somewhere in the new drawers and cupboards. But he needed no help recalling John McNeil. 'He'd come from a Third Division club, Torquay, and the first thing he did was drop all the wages by a pound across the board. That was a lot of money, and about half a dozen of us said we wouldn't sign – but eventually I was the last one holding out.

'It must have been the final week before the start of the season and Ruth was in hospital having our daughter Lynn. It was a Friday afternoon, I'd just been to see her and I went into the club. He says, "How's the wife – all right?" I says, "Fine." Then he says, "Are you signing this form?" and when I said no he says, "Right, I want the house back in two weeks." I had a club house on a fortnight's tenancy agreement. If you weren't signed on by the club they could have you out in two weeks.

'What could I do? She was in hospital about to come out with the baby. I told him I was signing under protest and I didn't speak to him for a fortnight.'

I'd assumed that the part-timers on the Bury playing staff were either youngsters on their way to turning full-time, like my father, or men the club thought weren't worth a contract. But speaking to Cyril alerted me to the existence of a third group: the substantial minority of players around the league who simply didn't want to sign away their independence. Tom Daniel was one of them. A versatile inside-forward, who could play alongside my father as well as on the right, he was also a draughtsman, earning a decent salary during the week, then picking up an extra wage on Saturday along with any bonuses.

He trained with my father on Tuesday and Thursday evenings, on the cinder car park in front of the main stand, and used to take Tuesday mornings off from work to play in the weekly practice match. Then he changed jobs and became a travelling salesman, so the practice match had to go. 'When Dave Russell took over from John McNeil as manager, he said, "Look you're going to have come full-time," and I said, "Well in that case I'd rather pack it in." So we just went on as we were.

'I remember we were in the coach going somewhere to play and I was sat next to Stewart. And he said straight out to me, "How much are you getting paid?" and I said I was getting £12 or whatever it was, and he said, "Oh, I'm getting £14" – or whatever his figure was. And I thought to myself, that's a bugger, isn't it, here I am pulling my bloody guts out and he's getting another couple of quid more than me.

'I must confess I was getting a bit niggly about it and I thought I'll go and see the manager. I said, "Is there any chance?" and he said, "No," so I said, "What about Stewart," and he said, "Well, if we want good young players from Scotland we've got to pay 'em." And at the time I accepted this, and it was only when I was going home I thought, well, what the hell's that got to do with me?

'Anyway, after a while I thought I'm not going to keep asking for a rise because I might get the other thing – y'know, shown the door.'

Anxiety about being shown the door rose as each season neared its end. It was then that the club produced its retained list, the players they planned to keep under contract for the following season and the terms which they were prepared to offer them. Methods varied from club to club. With some it was a slip in the season's final wage packet, or a registered letter. Elsewhere a list went up on the noticeboard outside the dressing room, or players were called in to see the manager one by one. Les Bardsley was the Bury captain when my father arrived, a hard wing-half who felt it was his responsibility to look after the young players in the side. He had them back for extra work in the afternoons, and faced down the Makepeaces of the Second Division for them on Saturdays.

At the end of the season he was as vulnerable as anyone in the group gathered at the door to the manager's office. 'It was bloody awful because you waited and somebody would come out and say, "What am I going to tell the wife now I've got the bloody sack?" Or they'd put you on the transfer list and you'd have to find out how much they wanted for you. They could put £5,000 on you and you'd think who's going to pay £5,000 for me? So you'd have to wait till they dropped it to nothing. And other clubs knew they would do that, so maybe for a few weeks you'd get no wages, unless you'd got another job.

'And if you were in a club house, they'd always be coming round with players they were wanting to sign, coming to have a look at your house. I threw them out, I said, "Sod off, I'm still here. Come back when I'm not here."'

In late 1952, none of this was of any concern to my father. He was starring in the first team on Saturdays and counting the months until the end of his joinery apprenticeship on his twenty-first birthday, when he could put his overalls back in the suitcase he'd travelled south with and start reporting for training on the Gigg Lane car park every day instead of two nights a week. By mid-October the headlines were proclaiming Bury's third win in a row, and the manager was doing his best to annex the credit for the signing of his star winger with a piece of blatant myth-making. In the versions he started giving to the newspapers, John McNeil had spotted my dad himself while on holiday in Scotland: 'I count his signing as the best day's work I ever did.' Willie Shanks, the diligent scout who'd sent Robbie Campbell for a trial with Bury months before my father and Eddie Archibald months after, wasn't mentioned.

Reading my way through his first season, my attention was caught by a couple of paragraphs boxed off from one of the match reports and headed 'BURY WINGER APOLOGISES':

> In the pre-match shooting-in Stewart Imlach, the young Bury outside-left, drove the ball into the crowd behind the goal: unfortunately it struck a young woman causing her some inconvenience. Imlach asks Ranger to express his apologies to the woman.

Ranger was the pen name of the Bury FC beat reporter.

I mentioned this during a weekend phone call to my mother as an amusing little episode. I was becoming, to my slight discomfort, the family authority on my father's career. Suddenly it was my job to supply historical snippets to the woman he'd lived with for forty-six years. There was an 'Ooh . . .' on the other end, then silence.

'What?'

'Well – I remember going once and getting hit with the ball.'

Ball meets girl!

'What, before you met Dad? Were you standing behind the goal?'

'Yes, I mean that's where we stood but . . .' This wasn't a historical snippet, it was a previously unrecorded sighting of Halley's Comet. My father had subconsciously picked out his future wife with a crisp half-volley during the warm-up, football's equivalent of the caveman's club over the head: there was years of psychoanalysis in this. 'But, no, no, it can't have been.' She was back-pedalling now, turning suddenly emphatic. 'No, I don't think I went to any first-team games before I met Dad, I think it was a reserve game.'

Thought? Hoped? Couldn't face the possibility? Why not? – she'd been convinced that my father had come back as an owl a few months after his death. Actually, I'd been pretty well convinced myself when she showed me the pictures she'd taken: the bird, perched on the kitchen counter by the bread bin, evidently waiting for her to put the camera down and get the kettle on. It had dive-bombed her a couple of times in the garden late at night, then invited itself in. And it did look remarkably like him.

The owl was one thing. The flying football of fate, though, she was distancing herself from. Pity. There was certainly no way of proving it. Perhaps it didn't need proving, perhaps it was enough not to categorically disprove it. Just to have it there as a pencil entry in the family compendium of coincidence.

They'd met officially at the Palais de Danse. 'The band was here' – I'm up in Formby for the weekend and she's mapping out the romantic battlefield in the living room – 'and we used to stand here. The footballers all used to stand across there when they came in, they always used to come in late. And all the girls, all the hangers-on, used to stand across there too. Well, you were common if you stood with the footballers. Common, a hanger-on.

'Anyway, as soon as the music started up he used to walk straight across the floor and they'd say, "He's coming!" and I'd say, "Oh God, I can't understand a word he says." He was a great dancer though, your dad. The only thing was, he needed the whole floor to himself – I used to get my heel caught in other fellas' turn-ups.' Perhaps misunderstanding the question, she said yes to his proposal of marriage.

My mother was a machinist at Bury Feltworks. It was her second job. She'd started at Clitheroe Shirtings when she was fourteen, sewing sleeves and collars onto children's school shirts. The girls weren't allowed to sew a whole garment for fear that they'd start making their own and selling them once they knew how. With her colleagues from the feltworks she had sat cross-legged on the floor of the Palais de Danse one week in 1953, hand-sewing the pieces of a giant gold carpet for the Coronation of Queen Elizabeth II.

My parents were due to be married in 1954, at the end of my father's second season. The date had been set for July, but in May he had to travel home suddenly for the funeral of his Grandad Dovey, the skipper of *The Snowdrop*. One day during his absence, my mother was called off the factory floor at the feltworks. All the women there were on piecework and any time spent away from the bundle of items stacked by the side of their machines was lost money. An interruption could only mean important news.

Waiting for her outside the factory were the Bury manager, Dave Russell, who'd taken over from John McNeil midway through the season, and his assistant Bert Head. They'd had an offer from Derby County for my father that was too good to turn down: £7,500 plus two players. Having decided to cash in on their most valuable asset, the club had quickly identified the most likely obstacle to completing the deal: the local girl looking forward to her July wedding and married life with the town's star footballer. Hence the emergency call. They wanted to break the news to her before her fiancé got the chance, and cast the prospective move in the best possible light.

'I remember going and sitting in Dave Russell's car and the two of them talking to me, and they just kept saying, "Derby's a lovely place, you know, there's no slums." That's all they kept saying, "There's no slums in Derby. And you'll get a hundred pounds when he signs on. Just think, you're getting married, think what you could do with a hundred pounds."' The standard signing-on fee at the time was actually £10. If the Bury manager was trying to persuade my mother with the promise of £100 from Derby either he was talking about an under-the-counter payment, or he was having her on.

'I remember going back inside and telling the girls, "There's no slums in Derby," and they were all saying, "That's a load of rubbish, there's slums everywhere."'

'Did he get the hundred pounds for signing on?' I asked her.

'I can't remember. I know he promised me a sewing machine when we got married – and he went out and bought a set of golf clubs.'

If Bury were keen to tie up the deal quickly, their Second Division rivals Derby County were even keener. My father agreed to the transfer over the phone from Lossiemouth, but the Derby manager, Jack Barker, insisted that the news be kept secret until his signature was on the contract, worried that if news got out that Bury were willing to sell, he'd have been outbid by a bigger club.

According to the papers there'd been interest in my father that season from teams offering between £15,000 and £20,000, substantial money for a young player who had yet to play two full seasons. Everton were among those that had been turned down; Burnley and Manchester United had both been to watch him. Derby had also made a previous offer of cash plus players. Dr J.S.M. McKay, a Bury board member, had stoked the interest with a livestock owner's pride: 'If we transfer that boy we'll want £10,000 for his heart to begin with. After that we'll start considering our price for him as a footballer.' The target of the offers would have known nothing about any of them, save for what he might glean from the occasional paragraph in the Bury *Times*.

Why Bury were happy to go along with Derby's request for secrecy instead of testing my father's value on the open market is a bit of a mystery. Certainly they seemed keen on one of the players Derby were offering in part-exchange, Norman Nielson, a big strong centre-half from South Africa. The makeweight in the deal was another South African, Cyril Law, who would slip conveniently into the left-wing spot vacated by my father.

Whatever the reasons behind it, the fact was that my father hadn't been offered a transfer so much as a done deal. Once the club had decided to sell he was given no chance to discover who else might be interested. He'd simply been summoned after terms between the two parties had already been agreed. My mother's parents had no telephone and the only conversation she was able to have with him about the proposed deal was during a call from Dave Russell's house, with the manager standing beside her. And so he signed. No private discussion with his fiancée, no face-to-face meeting with his manager. No trip to Derby to see the place or his prospective club. He simply signed.

The fact was, my father was no more likely to take on the authority of the Bury board than my mother was to refuse a move across the factory floor from the machine making dipstick-wipers to the one turning out felt covers for Ronson lighters. If he had resisted, Bury could simply have offered unacceptable terms for the following season and put him on the transfer list without the obligation to pay him.

'I was speaking to Enid about it the other day,' my mother told me – Enid was the wife of Eddie Gleadall, my father's inside-left partner and the best man at their wedding. 'She said Ted had an inkling that they wanted to sell him and he just came home one day and said, "I've signed for Scunthorpe." And she said, "Well, why didn't you say no?" He said, "You can't say no, if they want to get rid of you they'll get rid of you." So he just signed, without even speaking to Enid. That's just the way it was, if they wanted to sell you, that was it.'

Chapter Four

Club House:
Derby 1954–55

MY FATHER WOULD HAVE been unlikely to turn down a move to Derby County, even if he'd been given the choice. They may have been in the Second Division but they were a much bigger club than Bury, with a history spent almost entirely in the First.

If anyone had posted him the Derby papers, though, he might have had misgivings. I got there ahead of him and read the warning signs. Two weeks before his transfer, the club's retained list had been front-page news in the *Evening Telegraph*: RAMS PLAYERS GET CUTS IN PAY. Practically every man the club had decided to keep for the following season would be on lower wages. There's no surviving record of whether my father was guaranteed the maximum by Derby to sign for them. But they did promise him a house.

The club house stood solidly in the social tradition of tied-housing for key workers. Mill owners built estates or whole villages to accommodate large workforces; football teams kept a handful of properties for their itinerant employees. With players arriving, often at short notice in parts of the country they knew nothing about, it made sense for their employers to relieve them of the burden of finding somewhere to live so that they could concentrate on the game.

Young single players, like my father had been when he arrived in Bury from Lossiemouth, were put in digs, where landladies would provide them with clean sheets and cooked meals and the club with a steady flow of information on their out-of-hours activities. Houses were for married men.

It was sound business for the clubs – they could assemble a portfolio of property, get a rental return on their investment and help
contribute to a stable home life for their key performers. As Cyril
Fairclough knew, the eviction clause in the standard tenancy agreement also gave them a handy trump card in case of any disputes. For
plenty of players, though, club houses were perks of the job. When
I spoke to Eddie Baily, the great Spurs inside-forward who would
later play alongside my father at Nottingham Forest, he remembered
Tottenham owning half a dozen in a row on one north London
street. 'There was Ron Burgess, Les Stevens, Ernie Jones . . . six
of us all lived together, next door to each other. If we went out to
play a match and some of us come home and some didn't there was
a lot of trouble with the wives saying, "Why haven't you come home
with them?" Roedean Avenue in Enfield it was. They're all still
there.'

They used to leave their houses together every morning to catch
the same bus to training; teammates already synced to each other's
rhythms and routines before they'd reached the end of the street. I
wondered which player had moved into Eddie Baily's house when he
moved out. And who had moved into ours in Nottingham and
Coventry, and who'd lived there before us.

The club house is a historical footnote in the social development
of the game now. But, like the ones in Roedean Avenue, many of
them are still standing, retired from football these days, too small
and cheap and close to the ground ever to attract another playing
tenant; a network of anonymous family homes that have seen the
slowly evolving furniture choices of several generations of a single
team's players. Perhaps we need a plaque scheme to mark them out
from their identical neighbours.

In 1954, though, Derby County, on club houses as on wages,
seemed to be economising. My mother and father had been married
in mid-July, meaning that he hadn't joined his new teammates for

the start of pre-season training. After a week's honeymoon on the Isle of Man, the newlyweds arrived in Derby to begin married life as lodgers. With the season about to start, they were asked to share with the team's centre-half and his family while the club found them somewhere permanent to live.

My mother had been dreaming of a small place of their own in Bury. Instead they had only a bedroom to themselves, with no lock on the door. 'There was Ken Oliver and his wife, their two children and her elderly mother. Their lad, Keith, was a little sod. Dad nearly murdered him a couple of times because he kept coming in. We hadn't brought much with us from Bury because we didn't have much. But there was a mirror and hairbrush that I'd had a long time and he smashed the mirror. We used to come back and find him bouncing up and down on the bed. He was just a little lad, I suppose.' They made friends with Terry Webster, the young Derby goalkeeper, and his wife, who'd been on the club's housing list themselves and had given up waiting.

The problem with the house my parents had been promised was that it was occupied by another player, the captain, Bert Mozley. Bert was a Derby legend. Born in the town and apprenticed at the Rolls-Royce engine factory, he'd signed for the club after the Second World War and racked up over 300 appearances for them at right-back. He might have won more than his three caps for England if it hadn't been for injury and the emergence of Tottenham's Alf Ramsey. He was the epitome of the local boy made good, at a club filled with local boys. When he joined in 1946 there were seven first-team players born within a fourteen-mile radius of the Baseball Ground.

In 1954, at the age of thirty-one, Bert Mozley was approaching the dilemma that all professional athletes face at the end of their accelerated career trajectories: what to do next. If the status conferred by his captaincy of the club turned up no better offers, he knew he could always go back to work for Rolls-Royce. Then, out of the blue, he got the offer of a job in Canada, running a hotel. It was one of a chain owned by a man called George Davis, who'd played for Derby at the turn of the century before emigrating to make his millions. Bert had met him on an England tour of Canada a few years earlier, and now the old ex-Ram was offering him the chance of a new life in Calgary.

Taking the job, though, would mean asking for his release from the club. 'I had a meeting with the board of directors and I told them what I thought, and they said, "Well, we wish you all the luck in the world, Bert, and if Derby ever come over we hope we can stay in your hotel." Then when it came time to pick up my benefit from them they said, "Oh no, you broke your contract." I said, "I came to meet you in the boardroom and you gave me your permission," but they said, "No, you broke your contract so you don't get the money."'

Benefit money was a sort of loyalty bonus that built up in annual increments, in recognition of footballers' short working lives and lack of security: £500 after five years' service with the same club and another £750 after ten. These sums were taxable. Players could opt for a benefit match instead, but that was a gamble. The proceeds were tax-free, but the cost of staging the game had to be deducted, so the size of the crowd was crucial. Bad weather could easily cost a player his pension nest egg.

In practice, many clubs simply ignored the accrued benefit agreement, paying players what they felt they could afford, or paying nothing at all except to those who kicked up a fuss. Bert Mozley, a one-club man his entire career, was a season away from his £750 benefit. The board refused to pay it, or even the portion of it he'd earned. 'They offered me a hundred pounds. A hundred pounds after ten years' service, nearly. I was really disappointed. You play your heart and soul out for the club in the town you was born in

– I loved playing for Derby County – and that's what they do to you.'

The man refusing Bert Mozley his benefit money was the chairman, O.J. Jackson, who ran a construction business and also owned a large store in the centre of Derby. His involvement with the club brought him more public recognition than either of his business ventures, but he was no closer to the captain of his team than he was to his site foreman. 'He lived up past me and I remember one week we were playing in London and we had to catch the one o'clock train on the Friday. I got down to the bus stop and it was pouring with rain. He came past in his car with his wife and they just waved. He wouldn't stop to pick you up – and we were going to the same place. Once when we got back late after a night game his housekeeper who'd come out with the car said, "Oh Mr Mozley, we'll drop you off," and oh, he was mad, he didn't like that.'

As Bert Mozley's dispute with the board dragged on through the season, my parents were without a house of their own. On the field my father was having an anonymous time in an underperforming team. Derby, who had spent all but one of the previous twenty seasons in the First Division, were struggling in the bottom half of the Second. Bert handed over the captaincy to my dad for the day when Derby played Bury in October. He scored in a 2–2 draw, but missed a couple of chances that could have won the game and perhaps made him feel that the move had been less of a mistake. Mistake is my word, though. He wouldn't have looked on it as a mistake. How could he? He hadn't been party to the process that had taken him there.

Just before Christmas 1954, Bert Mozley was finally granted his release by the Derby board, although they retained his registration in case he should ever return to England. He was due to sail to Canada on 8 January 1955, with his wife to follow once he was settled. Aware that public sentiment was on Bert's side, the directors issued a statement a few days before his departure: 'Had Mozley completed his service he would have received his second full benefit of £750. However, when he asked for his release so that he could sail for Canada . . . he stated that he would leave even if permission were not granted. The directors have allowed Mrs Mozley to stay on in a club house and rent free for a period of three months even though the house is urgently required for another player.'

Three months. It looked as though the board's self-proclaimed magnanimity was going to keep the Imlachs out of their first marital home for almost the entire season. Then Derby signed another Scot and their priorities changed.

'They gave the house to Jock Buchanan.' My mother's voice rose with indignation as she broke the fifty-year-old news to me. Buchanan was an inside-forward from Clyde, one of a handful of signings Jack Barker made over the course of the 1954–55 season as Derby looked increasingly likely to go down into the Third Division. By February a certain amount of desperation was setting in. A new forward who could save the club with a clutch of late-season goals would be a godsend. And if the only way to get him was to promise him a house – even if it was the same house that had been promised to the last prospective saviour of the club six months earlier – then so be it.

My mother was distraught. Jack Barker told her not to worry, he'd find them another house. 'Well, he showed us this horrible place. Bert Mozley's was a nice modern house. This was old and dark and dingy, it was awful. None of the other players were living in a house like that.'

I knew this story, it had had a few airings over the years. This was the day my mother attacked the manager of Derby County with her handbag.

'What made you hit him?'

'We were in his car – Jack Barker's – and he said, "Right what d'you think?" and I said, "No I don't like it." Well he started prodding me, saying, "You'd made up your mind before you went in there that you weren't going to have that house," so I just whacked him. I says, "Don't you point at me. You might be his boss but you're not mine." I can't believe I did that.'

Looking at her I can't quite believe it either.

'I whacked him and got out of the car, and of course Dad had to get out and follow me. We went straight round to Terry Webster's and the two of them sat down and drafted his transfer request.'

Jack Barker was already under pressure from the board over results. The last thing he needed was to have to explain away a sudden transfer request from a player he'd signed at the start of the season to help improve them. The following day he called round to apologise, but it was too late. My father may have known his place in football's feudal hierarchy, but his sense of right and wrong was absolute. Once he'd made up his mind, the keys to the chairman's house with fixtures and fittings included wouldn't have been enough to change it.

The uncurious *Evening Telegraph* reported the barest facts: 'Imlach, who was married last summer, told us that he had decided to seek a move because of housing difficulties. Mr Cyril Annable, the Derby County Secretary, had no comment to make about the reason for the winger's request.'

This was typical provincial sports journalism of the time. The football beat writers almost always operated under a pen name – Ranger, Free Forester – and in exchange for the access granted to them by the club, they contrived to overlook almost everything which that access allowed them to see. My father finished the season in the reserves as a result of his transfer request, losing the appearance money that made up a substantial portion of a first-team player's wage, and missing the last few defeats that made relegation a certainty. The Friday after all hope of staying up had been lost, the inevitable announcement from the Baseball Ground was the signal for the *Evening Telegraph* headline writers to give full reign to their creativity: 'JACK BARKER RESIGNS: POST TO BE ADVERTISED'.

My father's dispute with Derby County was personal and particular. But it coincided with a growing dissatisfaction among footballers in general. The same week that he put in his transfer request, the Players' Union went public with the latest in a series of attempts to persuade the Football League to improve their contracts. Jimmy Guthrie, the union chairman, had sent the league a document containing the signatures of almost all his 2,500 members, attacking the way they were treated by their clubs. It made all the newspapers, but it made no real difference.

The problem for Guthrie and his colleagues was that the men who ran the Football League viewed the Players' Union as an organisation in the same way that the men who ran the clubs looked on their players individually: with the arrogance of owners. That was no real surprise, of course, since the men who ran the Football League *were* the men who ran the clubs.

There was a Joint Negotiating Committee comprising the Union, the Football League and the FA. But the two governing bodies flatly refused to discuss the players' key demands. In April 1955 Fred Howarth, the League Secretary, wrote to the union prior to a meeting of the JNC: 'With regard to the agenda, I am to inform you that the league has decided to take no part in any discussion with regard to item 5, namely, Contract of Service, if the points to be raised are such as have already been dealt with.' The union wrote back outlining suggested areas of debate. Howarth told them that most of the items had already been covered, 'in some cases more than once'. Any attempts to raise the banned issues at meetings, he warned the union, would see the proceedings closed down by the chairman.

The maximum-wage system had been in effect since 1901, and by 1955 it had been nudged up to £15 a week by negotiation and government arbitration, usually in the face of opposition from the league; the £10 signing-on fee was as old as the maximum wage and hadn't increased in over half a century. Bonuses were the same £2 for a win and £1 for a draw that players had earned in 1920, the year they were introduced.

But in talking to my father's contemporaries I'm struck by how little any of it seems to have been a source of real dressing-room dissent. With a cup of tea on the arm of the sofa and the scrap albums out, it would only take a mention of the retain-and-transfer system to set them off on a litany of ancient complaint and pickled grudge. But when it came to wages there seemed to be some kind of extension of the wartime spirit in effect – they were all in it together, working-class lads banging their heads on the same ceiling.

Except for those who went abroad. In that summer of 1955, while my father was waiting to see who might buy him from Derby, Eddie Firmani left Charlton for Sampdoria in a move that must have echoed round the dressing rooms of the Football League like a drill through a bank-vault wall. It broke the British transfer record, which had stood since 1951 when Sheffield Wednesday bought Jackie Sewell from Notts County for £34,500. Sampdoria paid only £500 more to Charlton for Firmani, but it was the comparison of personal terms that dropped jaws.

Sewell had received the standard £10 signing-on fee, and as Britain's most expensive player was presumably earning the maximum wage of £15 a week and £13 during the close-season. Firmani's signing-on fee was £5,000, or roughly six years' salary for

Sewell. That was before his weekly wages of £100, the free apartment, the generous bonuses – and the knowledge that when his contract expired, after two years, he'd be free to sign with whom he pleased.

A couple of months after Firmani's transfer, Jimmy Guthrie told this tale of two footballers to the TUC annual conference in Southport. Against the wishes of some of its committee members, the Players' Union had decided to affiliate to the Trades Union Congress in search of increased leverage against the immovable objects of the FA and the Football League.

Guthrie opened his speech with a piece of melodramatic grandstanding:

> Mr Chairman and delegates, I stand here as a representative of the last bonded men in Britain – the professional footballers. We seek your help to smash a system under which now, in this year of 1955, human beings are bought and sold like cattle. A system which, as in feudal times, binds a man to one master or, if he rebels, stops him getting another job. The conditions of the professional footballer's employment are akin to slavery.

His performance went down well in the hall, but badly outside it. Many of Guthrie's members were more upset by his description of their contracts than the contracts themselves. The footballers of the '50s were heroes of the working class. Hundreds of thousands paid to watch them every week. Their photos were in the new magazines, hand-coloured like American film stars. These pictures and the one being painted by their union leader couldn't both be true. Faced with a choice, plenty of players preferred the inaccurate flesh tones they saw in *Charles Buchan's Football Monthly* to Jimmy Guthrie's grim black and white.

* * *

Derby finished the 1954–55 season as they had the previous one, by announcing wage cuts across the board. Despite having had his request for a transfer granted by the club, my father's name appeared on the list of retained players; if he wasn't sold by June when his old contract was due to run out, he'd have to sign the new one for less pay. A week after the announcement he played his final game for Derby County, a friendly against Third Division Chesterfield to raise money for the Derbyshire FA. They lost 7–0.

Chapter Five
Two Games against Manchester United

DRIVING NORTH. I DON'T own a car so hiring one usually means an occasion. The last time I'd set off out of London up the M1 it had been a midnight scramble to find a rental place open, after the call from the hospital to say he was dying. I remember passing the overnight road crews resurfacing the carriageway and wondering why they were still out working. Had nobody told them? Listen, lads, he's never going to drive this stretch of motorway now, you might as well pack up and go home.

This time, though, I ignored the left fork onto the M6 and kept going – back to West Bridgford where I was born, part of Nottingham's post-cup final baby boom.

My parents had landed there as grateful refugees from Derby in the summer of 1955, and settled into a club house a brisk walk from Forest's City Ground. This is where he'd been happiest, where he'd stayed the longest – five seasons – and where he'd played his best football. I was met in reception by Les Bradd, who had been a player across the River Trent at Notts County when my father returned to Nottingham to begin his coaching career there in the late '60s.

Les was a classically strong, Yorkshire-bred centre-forward, who still holds County's goal-scoring record. Now he works for their neighbours and rivals as Corporate Sales Manager. Forest's history is part of his patter, part of the spiel he uses to entertain clients on match days. Every picture on the wall, every cup and pennant in the trophy cabinet comes with a verbal caption. There's nothing glib about the delivery though, he's articulate and enthusiastic – you can tell it all still matters to him – and his passion for the game glints in the historical detail: here are Frank and Fred Forman, the first brothers to play together for England, in the 1898–99 season, their caps behind glass in the boardroom; here's Forest's first cup-winning team from 1897–98, proudly showing off the trophy – *before* the game.

It's a great story. At the photographer's request, Nottingham Forest and their opponents, Derby County, had each posed with the cup before the game kicked off so that there'd be a suitable picture of the winners whatever the result. Perhaps he had another engagement to get to and couldn't wait until the final whistle. Or perhaps it had more to do with nineteenth-century standards of photographic etiquette. Portraits were formal occasions demanding one's best clothes, so the idea of showing the teams in their post-match disarray might have offended late-Victorian sensibilities. And the story didn't end there. In black and white, the photographer feared that Forest's red shirts wouldn't stand out sufficiently well from the foliage in the background, so he had them borrow Derby's white tops for the picture.

Fabulous. So Nottingham Forest's first great moment of triumph was captured for posterity before the fact and in the colours of the opposition. Somewhere, I presume – unless the wet plate was destroyed at the time for the sake of propriety – is a fading team picture of Derby County posing in proud anticipation with a trophy they never won.

From reception onwards the walls at the City Ground are largely covered in the bright red of the Brian Clough era, and on the basis of proportional representation there's no arguing with a League Championship and consecutive European Cups. Among all the colour, the black-and-white images from the '50s stand out like newspaper front pages. In the Legends Room – a members-only club where fans can get a drink and a chicken balti pie for £2 surrounded by Forest history – there's a giant blow-up of the 1959 FA Cup-winning team.

But something's wrong with the symmetry. My father's in his usual place, seated at the front, but the hierarchy of heights has been interrupted to place Roy Dwight in the middle of the back row, dwarfed by centre-half Bob McKinlay on one side and goalkeeper Chic Thomson on the other. Les tells me it was the only place Dwight could stand to hide the thigh-high plaster cast on the leg he'd broken at Wembley after scoring Forest's first goal in the final. Behind glass in the Trophy Room there's a replica of the cup itself, small and bottom-heavy so that it looks like an ornamental coffee pot, and a framed copy of the cheque representing Forest's share of the Wembley gate receipts: £11,402 6d, dated 11 June 1959 and drawn on Barclays Bank, Pall Mall.

For me the most precious object in the cabinet is a football. Yellow with white laces and a desiccated bladder rattling inside, it was last kicked in October 1957. I'm not the only person who would think it valuable: in black ink on the leather panels are the signatures of the Busby Babes, fresh out of the bath in the away team dressing room. The game had been so sublime that Forest's trainer Tommy Graham had asked both sets of players to sign the match ball.

My father's autograph is there, compact and slanted, in his playing position – up in the top left corner of a panel that the centre-forward Tommy Wilson has signed bang in the middle. The only questionable signature is Matt Busby's. Instead of black ink it's in green Biro, with his title, 'manager', in brackets underneath. It's too ludicrous to be a forgery, so perhaps the fountain pen ran out, or one of the United players held onto it after he'd signed and Tommy Graham was left scrambling for whatever came to hand when the great man emerged. The Forest trainer gave the ball away to be raffled at some fundraising event or other and it had come back to the club on permanent loan from the family of the winning ticket-holders.

Coming early in the season, the match itself decided nothing, led to nothing, wasn't a turning point or a launch pad for either side; it was a league game, one of forty-two. Yet without the leverage of significance, it became a classic. Not years later, once the selective collective memory had edited it down into twenty minutes of brilliantly flickering highlights, but instantly and universally. It must have been an extraordinary match.

1957–58 was my father's third season with the club. Forest were newly promoted from the Second Division, Manchester United were the defending champions. The newcomers had made a great start — they were level on 17 points with United, the pair of them lying third and fourth in the league. For the Forest players the visit of the Busby Babes would have been like getting their first-class ticket punched, validation of their arrival in the top flight.

The same seems to have been true for the spectators. On the day of the game the queues outside the City Ground began at eight in the morning. An hour before kick-off there were more than 47,000 fans inside, 3,000 on the running track around the pitch because there wasn't room on the terraces. Benches were brought over from the cricket ground at Trent Bridge to seat them. The weather was implausibly warm and sunny for mid-October. Then the game began. The match reports were uniformly rapturous, a media conspiracy of praise and enjoyment. They read like a sort of nostalgia for the present, as if the entire press box had been briefed on the strictly embargoed knowledge that games like this wouldn't be around for much longer. As though some kind of pre-Munich heightening of the senses had sharpened everyone's appreciation for the simple beauty of a well-played game of football.

One of the best accounts of the match appeared in the Manchester *Guardian*, under the byline 'Old International'. The writer was Don Davies, who would die four months later in the crash at Munich.

For one traveller at least this was the perfect occasion; a case where the flawless manners of players, officials and spectators alike gave to a routine league match the flavour almost of an idyll.

There was the tingling sense of a great occasion . . . Rarely, if ever, has expectation of a football treat been more thoroughly roused; rarely, if ever, has it been so quickly and completely satisfied.

Before play had been in progress five minutes one could detect the four cornerstones of Forest's recent successes. These were, in emergence, the two wing half-backs, Burkitt and Morley, the veteran schemer and strategist Baily, and that bundle of fiery endeavour with a keen football brain and a long, raking stride, Imlach.

He has a strongly marked gift for intelligent roaming, in pursuance of which he once crept up behind Blanchflower unawares and gave that Irish international the shock of his life by suddenly thrusting a grinning face over his shoulder, the while he nodded a long, high centre from Quigley unerringly home.

That headed goal from my father just after half-time was Forest's equaliser, Liam Whelan having put the visitors ahead early in the game. Twelve minutes later Dennis Violet scored again for United and, despite a last half-hour of sustained home pressure, 2–1 was the final score. Afterwards the managers, the players and the press lined up to pay tribute to themselves, each other and the game. 'I'll have to cast my mind back some way to recall a game as good,' declared Matt Busby, who had just led his team to successive League Championships and into the European Cup. 'Give me such matches and I might forget we didn't get the points,' said the Forest manager, Billy Walker.

Frank Swift, the legendary Manchester City goalkeeper turned sportswriter, summed up in the *News of the World* the following day: 'The luck then to United. The glory to Nottingham Forest. And my thanks to both teams for a match which was a credit to British football.'

Wow. I'd always thought of the 1959 FA Cup Final as my father's finest hour – hour and a half – and the '58 World Cup in Sweden as his biggest honour. I'm certain that he had too. But World Cups and FA Cups were special by definition. They were what players strived for. Games like this one were what they played for, the reason they played at all. Not for the glory or the win bonus, but for the simple routine joy of it. Careers only consist of highlights in retrospect; in real time they're a rolling, rhythmic continuum: this week, next week, midweek. And for my father this game against Manchester United was on a direct line stretching all the way back to the ones on the square in Lossiemouth. The crowd was bigger and the setting grander and everybody's kit matched, but the elements that mattered were all the same.

I hadn't consciously made the connection before, but as I read about the United match my mind leaped forward too – to the 1990s when I was in America covering the NFL. The coach of the Buffalo Bills, Marv Levy, was a man of my father's vintage who was perpetually being beaten by Manchester United, or the gridiron equivalent. His teams went to four Super Bowls and lost them all. But that's not what sparked my memory of him. It was what he used to say to his players as they emerged from the locker room before a game: 'Where else would you rather be?'

Pre-season, play-offs, Super Bowl, it didn't matter to Marv – or rather it all mattered equally: 'Where else would you rather be, men – than right here, right now?' Compared to the chest-beating war cries we heard every week on the satellite feed from NFL Films it sounded refreshingly old-fashioned, like something out of a

1940s film. It became an office catchphrase, wearily ironic in an edit suite of empty pizza boxes at two in the morning. We held Marv in great affection – we used him as a guest on live shows – and sent him up only gently, with respect. He was from a different generation to ours, and two generations removed from some of the young millionaires in his team. His unabashed sincerity seemed anachronistic, at odds with the brash mayhem of the modern game whooping and hollering its way past him towards the field, even as he offered his decent man's reminder to savour the privilege of being paid to play.

I think now that we were – I was – secretly embarrassed at how deeply he touched us with that rhetorical question. How he cut through the accumulated layers of cynicism that had formed since childhood into a thick crust over our enjoyment of sport, with a simple enquiry. I suspect the effect was the same on his team, regardless of age, race, social background or tax bracket. 'Where else would you rather be?'

My father never needed to ask himself the question. For the fourteen years of his playing career Saturday afternoons were taken care of. Whatever else might be happening in his life, personally or professionally, there they were at the end of the week, focal points of pure purpose.

When Crystal Palace released him in his thirties and he signed on for Dover and then Chelmsford in search of a game, a reporter asked him whether the Southern League wasn't perhaps a bit of a comedown for an ex-international. 'Bloody idiot,' he said, relating the story to my mother when he got home. He wouldn't have recognised the premise of the reporter's question. If you could play and you had the opportunity to play, why wouldn't you play? What else would you rather do on a Saturday instead? Where else would you rather be? I envied my father his certainties back down the decades. By the time I was in my thirties, Saturday afternoon had long since become the same shaped hole as Sunday, or – once I'd escaped my last newsroom and started working from home – any other afternoon of the week.

Christ, what a life. No wonder the clubs got away with treating players as slaves for so long. If bondage meant being forced to play Manchester United in front of 47,000 people, who in his right mind was going to volunteer for the escape committee?

That an unfashionable team like Forest, fresh out of the Second Division, could credibly take on the Busby Babes at their own beautiful game was in many ways thanks to the maximum wage and the hated retain-and-transfer system. Together they created a labour market that was a model of equal opportunity – but only for the clubs.

The low ceiling on players' earnings meant that a solvent Second or even Third Division outfit could match the wage scale of the top teams, where not everybody was on the maximum anyway. In fact, with appearance money making up a sizeable chunk of a player's weekly wage, there was every chance that he'd be better off playing regularly in the Second Division than turning out for the reserves at a club in the First. And if a player could legally earn no more at Old Trafford than he could down the road at Bury's Gigg Lane, or the City Ground in Nottingham, the financial imperative for moving to a bigger club was removed. Of course, there was always personal ambition – but retain-and-transfer took care of that.

The Nottingham Forest team that ran out to face Manchester United in October 1957 was undoubtedly a good footballing side, but in most other respects about as far from the ethos of Busby's carefully nurtured Babes as it was possible to get. Instead Billy Walker, a former England international and already a successful manager at Sheffield Wednesday, had assembled a sort of Magnificent Eleven: an unlikely blend of veterans, cast-offs, stars the bigger clubs thought were past their prime and younger players who, for one reason or another, hadn't realised their full potential elsewhere. It was as one of the last on this list that my father had arrived by train from Derby in 1955, to be met by the manager's assistant, Dennis Marshall.

'I'd just got in the office and I was taking my bicycle clips off when Billy Walker came in and said, "Don't take them off, I've got a little job for you." I said, "Do I get any taxi money? It doesn't make much of an impression, me arriving with me bike clips," and he said, "No, leave your bike here – get a bus from Trent Bridge."

'This lady came out first looking a bit flustered, and I was standing there holding a tin of paint because I'd had a bit of time to spare on the way up there. We started talking and I said, "I don't know what Billy Walker has told you about Nottingham Forest but we're not rich." Your mum said, "I don't care, we've got to get away from Derby." Then she told me the story – so I must have been the first person in Nottingham to know the business about the handbag.

'Foolishly, I caught a bus that terminated on the other side of the river. So there I am crossing Trent Bridge with a pot of paint trying to shepherd this handsome-looking couple to the ground, telling them, "Here's the Trent," like a tour guide. I took them into the boardroom and Billy Walker took them to lunch – which was very rare for him – and signed your father. I remember I had to type the forms up quickly because it was very close to the start of the season.'

Dennis Marshall is the curator of Nottingham Forest's anecdotal history. He could just as easily have been a sports journalist as a sports administrator, and he could just as easily have been a jazz journalist as a sports journalist. In fact, to start with he could well have been Forest's goalkeeper, had it not been for a bullet in the leg during the Second World War. He'd been at the club in various capacities since leaving school at the age of thirteen, finally settling into the custom-made post of personal assistant to Billy Walker, where he patrolled the swampy territory between what the manager told his players and the truth.

Since my father had no control over who bought his registration and where he was sent to play, all he could do was hope that Nottingham Forest would turn out to be a happier club than Derby. Dennis Marshall, with his tin of house paint and his bus fare for three out of petty cash, was the first sign that it would. Dennis's wife – Auntie Jean and Uncle Den, we grew up calling them – had the same-sized feet as my father and used to break in his new boots for him, unscrewing the studs and wearing them to do the house-work until they were soft enough to spare him the usual blisters. When Forest signed Jeff Whitefoot one close-season, it was my father who scaled the locked gates of the City Ground after Dennis realised that the keys to the Whitefoots' club house had been left in the deserted offices.

As I did the rounds of my father's surviving teammates, the one word that kept cropping up in relation to Forest was 'homely'. It was a small, friendly club, not long out of the Third Division when he arrived, and unique in the league in that it wasn't a limited company. It was run by amateurs, a committee of local worthies and businessmen, rather than an autocratic chairman who might view it as an outpost of his personal fiefdom. It could be a shock to the system for players coming from the upper echelons of the League. Chic Thomson, a clever and commanding goalkeeper, arrived from Chelsea in 1957 with a championship medal and a stronger sense of his own worth than some of his new teammates.

'I remember my first experience of travelling away with Forest. We had third-class return tickets. Bill Whare and I were going down the carriage saying to people, "Excuse me, excuse me – are these seats free?" We got it changed, a few of us, when we saw Rotherham were going north in the dining car and we were hunting for seats.'

Chic Thomson was one of a few shrewd buys that Billy Walker made on promotion to the First Division. To help get Forest out of the Second the season before, he'd flown in the face of opinion around the League to sign an ageing ex-international most people thought was ready for retirement.

Eddie Baily had been a brilliant inside-left both for England and the Spurs championship side of 1951. When Forest approached him five years later he was still in London, driving a three-ton truck and playing for Port Vale. 'I used to train in the morning at Leyton Orient, deliver these copper sheets in the afternoon, then go up on a Saturday to Port Vale and play,' Eddie told me, as though he were finally free, years after the fact, to let me in on the details of a fabulous con trick. He did pretty much the same for Forest, turning up at the Trent Bridge Inn on a Saturday just in time for the pre-match meal, then turning out, bandy-legged and balding, a few hours later to provide my father with the finest service of his career.

Along with having no real control over where he played, as a winger my father had only a limited amount over how well he was able to play. In the W formation of the '50s, the winger's job was to hug the touchline and wait to be fed. His inside-forward could make or break him. Just before Christmas 1956 Baily took over at inside-left when Billy Walker's other commuting veteran, the former Arsenal star Doug Lishman, missed his train. Over the next eleven games my dad scored ten goals and Forest racked up seven consecutive wins, dropping only two points between the New Year and March. It was enough to take them up.

'He done my running, bless his heart. Your dad was quick and he had a tremendous left foot. I was used to great wingers, I used to play with Les Medley who played for England with me – we represented England as a club pair. Your father was a similar type to Les. All my wingers got caps, I made 'em all internationals.' Eddie's cockney music-hall boasting is so matter of fact it almost sounds like modesty. But when he won his first Scotland cap the following season my father went out of his way to credit the contribution of his old inside-forward partner. By then, though, Eddie Baily was gone. Billy Walker had promised him and Doug Lishman under-the-counter payments of £400 if Forest were promoted. He hadn't delivered, and the two of them had confronted him.

'It was on a personal handshake between us. But when the time came he talked his way out of it – "It's illegal . . . I've been in the game a long time . . ." Yeah, that don't make no bleedin' difference. Doug was saying, "I'll kill the bastard." He was very upset. He was going to retire, start a little antiques business in Stoke, he said the money would come in handy. I wanted to re-sign, so I didn't want to make a fuss. In the end, the chairman got to hear about it and shortly into that season old Bill decided I'd be better off out of the way. That's when I signed for the Orient, which suited me – it was only a hundred yards from where I lived.'

Billy Walker may have promised illicit bonuses, but at Nottingham Forest he wasn't in a position to pay up. Even if he'd been able to get them sanctioned by the committee that ran the club, Forest had perhaps the most scrupulous secretary in the Football League. Noel Watson was an FA councillor, chairman of the FA Cup Committee, a qualified referee and a Justice of the Peace. Unmarried, his life dedicated to the game and to the club, he was the straitlaced yin to Billy Walker's slightly crooked yang.

'No, there were no bonuses at Forest,' Chic Thomson told me. 'At Chelsea, Ted Drake had an illegal system. If you'd had a good result, when you turned up on Monday he had a great big plate-glass window in his office and he used to bang on it – and when you walked in he said, "Oh, I owe you some money," and he used to give you an extra ten or twenty out of his drawer, so those things went on.

'When Ted Drake called me in to say Billy Walker at Forest had expressed an interest, he warned me, "He's a rogue – if he can get you for nothing he'll get you for nothing, so fight your corner." When I came to Forest I discovered that there was only Eddie Baily and I getting the top wage that first season, which was surprising.'

It was standard practice for clubs to skim the top few pounds off the maximum wage and call them 'appearance money' so that any player injured or in the reserves wasn't costing them more than absolutely necessary. My father, desperate to leave Derby and with limited experience of wage negotiations, would have accepted this happily. It was only canny veterans from the big London clubs who knew to insist on top money regardless of whether they were in or out of the team.

The fact that clubs well down the food chain like Forest could afford the maximum, although they did their best not to pay it, meant that the powerhouses of the First Division had healthy surpluses. Inevitably, some of them used the cash to subvert the system, even as their chairmen voted year in and year out to preserve it for the good of the game.

The classic example came to light at Sunderland in 1957. For years the club had been operating an illegal bonus system using money disguised in the annual accounts as payments for straw to cover the pitch in bad weather. Between them the League and the FA botched the commission of inquiry, exceeding their powers and handing out bans to players and directors that were later overturned in court. But the affair revealed the nonsense of a system that made criminals out of club officials, and brown envelopes the only means of paying players even a fraction of their true worth. In case any underlining were needed, the newspaper coverage of the scandal was punctuated by John Charles's transfer to Juventus. His reported signing-on fee was £10,000 – exactly a thousand times what a player could legally be paid in England.

But no club would volunteer to pay extra money out of sheer

munificence. A player had to ask. My father was in the quiet majority of footballers too naive or straight to think of posing the question. He wasn't even on the perfectly legal maximum wage except when he was in the first team. Still, he was in the first team most of the time, earning appearance money and win bonuses, which meant his income in the off-season, when he was paid only a summer retainer, would drop by around 30 per cent.

In early May, as the Forest groundstaff began painting the stands and preparing the pitch for the following season, my father crossed the river to Meadow Lane where the Co-op had its central depot close to Notts County's stadium. He signed on as a joiner and spent his summer as part of the maintenance staff, walking the floor with his toolbag over his shoulder, on hand for any repair jobs that might be needed by the bakers or the milkmen.

What? Every now and then some routine detail of his story seemed to slip its moorings and become unplaceably strange, like a familiar household object stared at for too long, or glimpsed suddenly from an unusual angle. Which generation was this we were talking about, again? What century?

Imagine this: the Chief Executive of the FA calling a plumber – and forty-five minutes later parting the net curtains to see David Beckham ringing his doorbell in overalls. It could never happen, except on television, a stunt for Children in Need or some yet-to-be-invented reality game show. But in 1955 it did happen, without generating a single paragraph in the papers. Alan Hardaker of the Football League opened his door one Saturday morning to find that the country's finest outside-right had come to fit his new sink: Tom Finney of England, Preston North End and Finney Bros plumbers and electricians. When he was at Tottenham, Eddie Baily had made a literal crossing of the divide between player and spectator. With fellow internationals like Bill Nicholson he spent his summers in the stands at White Hart Lane scraping a season's worth of accumulated grime off the tea bars where the fans queued for a half-time drink and a pie.

In truth there wasn't that much of a divide to cross. My parents' club house was in Abbey Road, a short walk from Dennis Marshall's and Bob McKinlay's and Jeff Whitefoot's. It was a nice enough neighbourhood, but nothing special. He walked to the ground on match days, a little earlier than the fans, and cycled to training during the week. If any of the seats at the City Ground needed mending he'd go home at lunchtime and come back with his tools. In the afternoons he could sometimes be seen out on his bike with a Wall's Ice Cream sign balanced on the handlebars. He had a sideline with the Notts County goalkeeper, Jimmy Linton, hanging them outside sweet shops and newsagents. My father and his teammates were a visible presence in the community, and if they were venerated it was from close range.

As a winger, he always had a closer physical relationship to the fans than most of his colleagues. At Bury one woman used to put toffees on top of the perimeter wall adjacent to where he lined up for the kick-off and, having no pockets, he was obliged to eat them to avoid giving offence. But there seems to have been something more to it than just proximity. Something about his demeanour that endeared him to the crowd.

After he died, I came across a fan's obituary on the Internet, a tribute to him from a man who'd paid the child's price at the turnstiles for that Manchester United game in 1957. Despite emigrating to Canada – or perhaps because of it – his emotional ties to the club remained strong and his memories fresh. As an eleven year-old, he'd stood on an orange crate in the same spot every week – bang on the halfway line opposite the tunnel where the players came out. He used to pray that Forest would win the toss and attack the Bridgford end first, so that my father would start on his wing.

On the days when the gods smiled, our hero 'Stewie' would sprint across and line up in what was then the traditional left-winger's position, hugging the touchline and inches from my nose, when time permitted signing autographs, having a few quick words of banter and always waving and giving a cheery nod to those of us close by.

Even when the reverse was true, the second-half line-up inevitably saw the same response from a player who always identified with his audience, and who appreciated the need to translate those skills and the ability he possessed into industrious efforts to induce entertainment.

'The thing is, Dad used to go . . .' My mother cast about for the right words. 'When he got on the pitch he'd go absolutely berserk,' was what she eventually settled on. I asked Den about it. 'He was very popular with them and I think it was because (a), he was very small, and (b) he was energetic – he looked like he was going to run after the ball.

'An outstanding thing about your dad was that, if it was a rainy afternoon and the kids were hanging about outside the dressing room wanting their autograph books signing, he would never walk past any of them. He'd stand there and sign them, and the pages were getting wet and he was getting wet and the other lads would be in the tearoom. I used to admire him for that and he used to say, "Well, they've all paid to come in" – a real old-fashioned way of thinking, and I'm sure there are some players that do it now.'

I'm sure there are, but not as sure as I am that I'm drifting off into hagiography as I try to get a sense of him as a working pro. He sounds like a sawn-off cross between Roy of the Rovers and Alf Tupper, the Tough of the Track. But this – as far as I can make out through the anecdote-filtering process that automatically kicks in when people speak to the sons of dead friends – is how he was as a player. At home he had a short temper to go with his quick humour, and almost no patience whatsoever. His small-town morality could curdle into petty indignation. Later in life, when he'd run out of major points of principle to make stands over, he'd make them over minor traffic infringements. He once terrified a teacher by tailing her all the way into her school car park to point out exactly how she'd misbehaved at a roundabout. But in the dressing room and on the field his role in the cast of characters that makes up every football team was the chirpy Scot. The decent, honest, humorous Scot, who always gave 100 per cent. And he was, and he did.

Until quite recently, Forest's 1959 Cup Final team had still been pretty much intact, sufficient numbers for a reunion. Now there were fewer alive than there were dead: just a handful of front rooms to visit. I felt a tremendous warmth in all of them, a welcome that was entirely down to him.

As ever the memories varied. The bus was late getting to Wembley on Cup Final day, or it was on time. The bonus for winning was £25, or £50, or nothing. But they were the variations among those who could remember. In Nottingham, as in Bury and Derby, there were the distressing cases of men with glorious pasts and no access to them. All history and no memory. It struck me that Alzheimer's might seem somehow less cruel in the young. To reach an age where the body fails and the accumulated memories of a lifetime are one's chief consolation, then to have them scattered irretrievably, as the mind fragments like a faulty hard drive, seems a double punishment.

The first sign was usually a wary wife, screening the calls. 'I'm awfully sorry . . .' the conversation would begin, ruling another batch of eyewitness testimony to my father's career inadmissible. I thought about leather balls with no waterproofing, multiplying their weight in the rain; every cross my dad pulled back from the byline arriving in the box like a blow to the head from a heavyweight.

Even among those who could remember, their wives could often remember more. I sat and watched men listen, open-mouthed, to stories about themselves which they could no longer haul to the surface, recited word for word by women who'd heard them repeated so often over the years that they knew them as well as nursery rhymes.

The first player I called on had his scrapbooks out ready for me. We sat and talked – generalities to start with. Then I asked him about playing against Manchester United, and the tragedy of Munich in 1958.

'I can't remember, what happened about Munich? Refresh my memory about what happened about Munich . . . Oh of course – I'd forgotten that . . . that had gone right out of my mind.'

But he was bluffing. He still didn't remember it. I could tell from the way he spoke and the look in his eyes. He carried on, doing his best to give me what I'd come for, and perhaps trying to reassure himself that this had been another momentary lapse. His wife chimed in, 'It's sad that you've come now, because he's got serious memory problems.' It was, but I was happy just to be there, having tea and spending time with men who'd spent so much time – and so intensely – with my father. I stayed and talked, listening to the stories he could remember, and steering round the rest.

Before the adrenalin had subsided that Saturday in October 1957 after the first, fabulous game against Manchester United, many Forest fans, and probably quite a few players, must have scanned the fixture list to underline the return game.

It was 22 February 1958, sixteen days after United's plane crashed at Munich on the way home from a European Cup tie in Belgrade, killing most of the side that had played at the City Ground. Forest were their first opponents in the League after the tragedy. The makeshift United team, under assistant manager Jimmy Murphy, had played one other game, beating Sheffield Wednesday in the fifth round of the FA Cup. The Forest line-up showed two changes from the team that had played four months earlier. Eleven Manchester United shirts – two of them worn by survivors, the rest bearing the numbers of the absent dead and injured – ran out in front of their home supporters. There were 66,123 people at Old Trafford, the biggest crowd since the war. Before the kick-off and at half-time the collection boxes were passed along the terracing and through the stands.

'They wanted us to take part in a memorial service before the match – you know, out on the pitch.' Chic Thomson had no cuttings around him, no props or prompts, he was back at Old Trafford, in the away team dressing room. 'We couldn't do that, we'd never have been able to play afterwards. It would have been too much for the players.'

In the end, it was decided to leave the two sides in their dressing rooms while the Dean of Manchester conducted an interdenominational service in a snowstorm that conjured up unavoidable images for anyone who'd seen the television pictures of the crash. Eventually the game began. After thirty-two minutes Forest's centre-forward, Tommy Wilson, chased a poor United clearance out to the right and cut the ball back to the edge of the box. As the play had moved to the other wing my father had instinctively drifted in from the left to fill the gap. From twenty yards out he drove the ball past Harry Gregg into a silent net. Forest 1 Manchester United 0. It was the first goal against them since the crash.

What was he feeling as he ran back to the halfway line? In my father's book, giving anything less than 100 per cent would have been an insult to the opposition and to the game. 'Just do your best,' that was his one-size-fits-all advice in any situation that called for fatherly guidance: 'Just do your best, Gaz, that's all you can do.' Knowing that he'd done his job to the best of his ability would have been my father's vaccination against any consequences. But actually scoring against the stricken team was something else. Did he play the rest of the match secretly hoping for an equaliser, something to save him from being the man who beat Manchester United when they were down? Whether he did or not, the equaliser eventually came. United played a surging, emotional second half, urged on by a single continuous roar of collective will from the crowd. Sixteen minutes from the end a corner dropped into the Forest penalty box and Alex Dawson forced it in. Forest held on for the last quarter of an hour and the game finished 1–1.

'All the league people came into our dressing room after the game, and Jimmy Murphy who was standing in for Matt Busby went round everybody and thanked us for our attitude during the game – that we hadn't sort of retired, if you like,' said Chic Thomson.

'What could you do? You had to play hard. Anything else wouldn't have been right.'

Chapter Six
World Cup

I'M UP IN THE ATTIC sorting through my dad's things. Envelopes, boxes, old suitcases pulled into parallelograms by the shifting weight of programmes and cuttings inside. The lack of order among the accumulated evidence of his career was always one of its big attractions. Nobody really knew what was up here nor exactly where it all was. He certainly didn't, and I don't remember him ever going up to look.

The jumble meant there was always the chance of a big find. Some item – perhaps a whole suitcaseful – that had been neglected for just long enough since the last time anyone else had stumbled across it, that it could legitimately be submitted for peer review as a new discovery. The whole business of going up into the attic had been a bit of an expedition, requiring stepladders, a torch and a careful tread on the crossbeams so as not to put a foot through the ceiling of my parents' room. Later on, my father converted it into an extra bedroom which became mine. But the suitcases and trunks were still shut away, under the eaves, and 'rooting about' – not far behind banging doors on my mother's list of antisocial behaviours – was discouraged for fear of startled birds taking a wrong turn out of the nest, and emerging, terrified, from the cupboard doors to flap and shit all over the furniture.

So, I'm up here sorting through his things. It's tempting to leave them as they are, all stashed in their various hiding places like a treasure hunt, so that we can keep discovering, enjoying and forgetting them in a happy amnesiac cycle. Somehow, though, I feel obliged. It doesn't get much pamphlet-space in the bereavement guides, but there's a shocking amount of housework that comes with death. Jumble-sale worries, bin-bag decisions, unfaceable wardrobes and toolboxes. So this is a bit of a cop-out; no rows of reheeled shoes to deal with up here, none of this stuff is going to the charity shop. It just needs sorting – club, country, programmes, photos – so that we know where to find him now that he's gone.

Here's an item I haven't seen before. Or if I have, it was long enough ago that I can happily rediscover it now. It's my father's player identity card for the 1958 World Cup, although the fashion for making the year an integral part of the title – Sweden '58! – hadn't yet caught on. According to the legend across the top of the oversized pink oblong in its plastic holder, this is the 'VIth World Championship – Jules Rimet Cup'. My father obviously hadn't had a recent photo to submit for it, because he's still sporting the classic '50s footballer look – slicked-back, centre-parted – when in fact he'd already swapped it by then for the crew cut I always remember him wearing, an inch-high, perfectly levelled brush of the kind only Japanese gymnasts seem to be capable of producing these days.

He used to say that he'd cut his hair to improve his speed, which I'd always taken as one of his jokes, but quite a few of the cuttings in the suitcase mention his obsession with weight and streamlining. This is a player who took the cane struts out of his shinpads to make them lighter and less bulky. He trained in spikes. He trained on the way to training and back again, on his bike. Billy Walker called him 'The fastest man, with the ball, that I have ever seen.' A year later at Wembley his haircut was distinctive enough that the Duke of Edinburgh stopped to ask him about it (it was only when he'd reached Chic Thomson three men along that he finally became exasperated with the number of Scots in the team). On his World Cup ID, though, my father still has his heavy, old-fashioned hair, and the corner of the photo is rubber-stamped FIFA, to guard against any foreign chancers turning up in Stockholm with their

With his parents and the local stationmaster, preparing to leave Lossiemouth for England, 1952.

Star centre-forward as mascot: my father – holding the ball – and the victorious Rob Roys.

The St James' youth club side. My father is on the far right of the front row, next to Sandy Reid.

(*Right*) A joiner's sense of geometry.
Warming up at Gigg Lane, 1953.

(*Below*) My father's first published
picture as a professional player,
in the week of his debut for Bury,
September 1952.

(*Below*) Scoring against
Doncaster Rovers, 1953.

VIᵀᴴ WORLD CHAMPIONSHIP - JULES RIMET CUP 1958
SWEDEN - SVERIGE

Identity card - Legitimationskort
Player - Spelare

Name: Imlach
Christian name: S.
Country: Scotland

FÉDÉRATION INTERNATIONALE
DE FOOTBALL ASSOCIATION
General Secretary

(P. T. O.)

With Aberdeen's Graham Leggat before
Scotland's warm-up game with Eskilstuna.

With the Scotland team, 1958.

Sunday Express back page, 3 May 1959.

Forest lampooned in the *Daily Express* for cashing in on the Cup Final.

Gordonstoun graduate and Lossiemouth boy: the Duke of Edinburgh shakes hands with my father before the match.

As Jack Burkitt lifts the cup, my father receives his medal from the Queen.

My father and Jack Burkitt with stationmaster Gordon Rogers on their arrival back in Nottingham.

The culmination of the Forest homecoming parade in Market Square.
My father is on the right, arm raised, behind the manager Billy Walker.

boots, an impenetrable accent and cleverly deconstructed shinpads like they'd read about in the papers.

An impostor would have got a very limited set of privileges for his trouble. On the back of the card in Swedish and English is written: *Free Admission to the Stadium – Standing Enclosure*. I'm sure I've never read that before, I would have remembered. I feel retrospectively insulted on his behalf, and at the same time reassured. At least it wasn't just the UK: footballers were second-class citizens all over the world. God forbid they should stray into the seated sections and start leering at the officials' wives. Better to keep them among their own kind where they'd feel more comfortable.

In 1958 Scotland had yet to be weighed down by a long and painful World Cup history; that is to say the painful World Cup history they had was still short. Their first appearance had been four years earlier in Switzerland, where they'd lost both their games – one of them 7–0 to Uruguay, the defending champions – and hadn't managed to score.

This time, though, they'd qualified impressively enough, getting through ahead of Spain, whom they had beaten 4–2 at Hampden Park. Optimism rose further with the news that the Scottish FA was to join most of the rest of the footballing world in appointing its first national team manager. It wasn't a full-time post, but the fact that they'd persuaded Manchester United's Matt Busby to take it on looked like a huge step forward. Player selection would still be in the hands of a committee, as it had always been, but here was a man with the authority to make a team in his own image despite the men in the blazers. Incidentally, it gave United the managership of two national teams – Busby's assistant Jimmy Murphy was in charge of Wales.

The appointment was reported on 16 January 1958. Three weeks later, and two days before the date of the World Cup draw in Stockholm, came the Munich air disaster. Matt Busby was gravely ill; Jimmy Murphy had missed the trip, staying behind for Wales's play-off game against Israel in Cardiff, which would clinch their place in Sweden.

It was one of those innocent chains of events that form themselves into cruel or miraculous shapes only after tragedies, when they are revealed as having saved a life, or cost one. There should have been no good reason for Jimmy Murphy to be on international duty in February 1958. Qualifying had finished the previous year and Wales had failed, coming second in their group behind Czechoslovakia. Israel, meanwhile, had qualified without playing a game. Four nations in their section – Egypt, Indonesia, Sudan and Turkey – had refused to play them, leaving them to top the Asia and Africa group by default. FIFA called an emergency meeting at which it was decided that Israel would face a play-off against one of the second-placed European teams. Wales were drawn out of the hat. So Jimmy Murphy owed his life indirectly to the burgeoning tensions in the Middle East, and Wales went to Sweden as the representatives of Asia and Africa.

It was the first and only time that all four home nations qualified for the World Cup finals. And Scotland again found itself as the only one of the four without a manager. The hospital reports from Munich made it clear that Matt Busby wouldn't recover from his injuries in time to lead the team. The Scottish FA reacted by announcing a review of World Cup travel arrangements; the possibility of getting to Sweden by sea and rail instead of flying was to be investigated. There was no mention of finding a replacement manager. Instead, Scotland were led into the 1958 World Cup by a sponge-man.

'Dawson Walker was the trainer at Clyde, he was more for injuries, y'know. He'd never played the game, certainly not as a professional. We were possibly the only nation there without a manager or a coach, the only country that didn't have a figurehead like that.'

Eddie Turnbull has preserved his scorn intact for the best part of half a century. My father was twenty-six when he went to Sweden, young enough to have watched the great Hibs inside-forward in a wartime exhibition game in 1943 as a schoolboy. By 1958 Turnbull was a 35-year-old wing-half and knew he would only ever play in one World Cup. He's eighty-one now, but the baritone that intimidated generations of footballers in his time as player and then manager at Hibernian and Aberdeen retains its force. And his memory is clear and bitter. 'We had to do it ourselves. I was the oldest in the group, I think, and we had to do training sessions. It was ludicrous really, the preparation we had.'

The decision to travel to Sweden without a manager was attacked from all sides. Peter Black, writing in Scotland's *Weekly News*, denounced the SFA hierarchy: 'I can't see a soul on the selection committee with either the time or the qualifications to take our World Cup hopes and fashion them into a well-disciplined outfit with a proper plan of campaign. I warn you that unless we can induce a change of mind in the selectors, Sweden 1958 will be Switzerland 1954 all over again. And what a horrible thought that is.' The SFA responded by withdrawing the paper's credentials for the upcoming competition.

The members of the selection committee were themselves chosen from the ranks of Scottish club chairmen and directors. 'Potato merchants and what have you,' Eddie Turnbull calls them, 'men who'd never played the game at any level whatsoever.'

It had taken my father longer than some people expected to come to their attention. As early as 1953 he'd been touted as a likely name to be in the Scotland squad for a home international against Wales, but the call hadn't come. In the end it was Matt Busby who recommended to the selectors that they take a closer look. A contingent from the Scottish FA travelled down to watch him in a match against Leicester City at Filbert Street in October 1957. It was the week after that legendary—ordinary game between Forest and United, so perhaps it did lead to something after all. He played well in a Forest win, and after that the selectors kept an intermittent eye on him through the winter.

In the first week of February 1958, he was named in a Scotland eleven to play a World Cup trial game at Easter Road in Edinburgh against a Scottish League team. At Lossiemouth secondary, the headmaster made the mistake of confiding the news to some of the senior pupils and had to abandon the school day shortly afterwards, once the news had spread from classroom to classroom.

Six years into his professional career my father was making his first senior competitive appearance in Scotland. He played superbly, crossing for Mudie and Currie to head Scotland's first two goals and scoring the winner himself in a 3–2 victory over the League. The next morning's Scottish press was ecstatic: 'IMLACH IS SCOTLAND'S WING DISCOVERY,' 'IMLACH – A FIND'. Found? Discovered? By whom? The man they were talking about as some walk-on wonder was an English First Division player.

The truth was that the majority of his countrymen had never heard of him. Most of the other 'Anglos' in the squad, men like Preston's wing-half Tommy Docherty and the Liverpool goalkeeper Tommy Younger, had made a name for themselves in Scotland first. Without television to spread the news, my father's rise from the Second Division with one of England's less glamorous clubs would have had an audience not much wider than the readership of the *Northern Scot*. And so his first senior game in Scotland was as an alien, an exotic import. Lossiemouth, in any case, was a place even Scots might struggle to place on the map. The *People's Journal* ran a series of features on him: 'THE WORLD CUP STAR FROM FOOTBALL'S BACKWOODS'.

He was named in the World Cup squad of twenty-two and in the team to play Hungary at Hampden Park in May 1958. It was the first in a pair of warm-up games that would see them head to Sweden via Warsaw to play Poland. Before the match two telegrams were delivered to the dressing room – one from my mother: 'All the luck in the world, Darling', the other from Lossiemouth Town Council, sending him the entire community's good wishes. As one councillor pointed out, there was a precedent for this sort of municipal extravagance – they'd done the same with a Lossie émigré to South Africa on his hundredth birthday, and later paid for his ashes to be brought home and scattered on the Moray Firth.

The Hungarians weren't the same side who'd rewritten the rules of the international game five years earlier with their dismantling of England at Wembley, but they were still considered top-class opposition. My father played well in a 1–1 draw and the squad headed off for a training camp at Turnberry. Any misgivings the players might have had about being managerless were more than likely outweighed by the honour of representing their country in a World Cup. More to the point, there was little they could do about it – the administrators ran the game; they just reported at the specified times and dates, and played.

At Turnberry, though, there was discontent when they learned that they would receive no out-of-pocket expenses while they were in Sweden. The established rate for foreign games was £2 a day, but the Scottish FA, perhaps worried about how well the team might do and how long the trip might last, announced that it wouldn't be paid. Instead, if any player wanted Swedish kronor to spend during the competition he'd have to ask for an advance which would be deducted from his match fees on return to the UK.

The players protested, and the sportswriters, probably with a guilty eye on their own expense accounts, were sympathetic. The SFA, however, claimed they'd be breaking 'an international agreement' if they relented. The international agreement, it turned out, was a pact they'd made with the football associations of England

and Wales that none of them would pay per diems. England and Wales, though, changed their minds; the SFA didn't.

For men on the fringe of selection, like Falkirk's right-back Alex Parker, the trip suddenly became a fraught financial proposition. 'I played against Paraguay, didn't get a game against Yugoslavia, didn't get a game against France. Now, you got £50 a match if you played, £30 if you were a reserve. When we got back and my expenses were deducted, I got a cheque off the SFA for £14.' Tommy Docherty, who lost the captain's job to Tommy Younger in the run-up to the competition, didn't play at all. When he got home he owed the SFA money.

The squad made primitive attempts to compensate. They approached Swallow, makers of expensive raincoats, but Swallow weren't interested in seeing their garments on the shoulders of footballers, even internationals. In the end they settled for a lambswool jumper each off another company, which they had to model for a squad photograph. With their SFA blazers and flannels and their free sweaters, the players flew to Warsaw. Morale was good. It improved when they beat Poland 2–1, and comfortably survived the food and the sightseeing trip laid on by the Ministry of Tourism – to Warsaw's Jewish ghetto to see where thousands had perished during the Nazi siege.

By contrast the small steel city of Eskilstuna – often called Sweden's Sheffield according to the 1958 World Cup press guide, although it doesn't say by whom – rolled out the red carpet. Scotland's two coaches were stopped at the city limits by a fleet of vehicles with the mayor's at the head. The committee men stepped down onto the street to hear a speech of welcome, then the procession, with police outriders sounding their sirens, was escorted to a civic reception.

The choice of Sweden as host country hadn't gone down well in South America. Since the '54 World Cup had been held in Switzerland there were complaints of a European bias. FIFA, though, was less concerned with alternating between the continents than having a neutral venue that offended as few post-war sensibilities as possible. And in 1958 there was to be the consolation of live television.

Actually, 'live' had yet to establish itself as the adjective of choice for these instantaneous broadcasts. In both the *Radio* and *TV Times*, the listings boasted of World Cup games 'direct' from Sweden. The BBC showed the opening ceremony, a modest fly-past by the Swedish Airforce in front of the King, followed by the first match, Sweden versus Mexico. The game kicked off at 2 p.m. with commentary by Kenneth Wolstenholme. At 2.45 there was *Gardening Club* with Percy Thrower, then the second half of the match at 3.00. Without a studio to fall back on, the BBC had the Swedish television pictures to broadcast and nothing else; evening games during the week filled the half-time gap with fifteen-minute news bulletins. Still, this was a massive leap forward. There had been cameras in Switzerland, but the 1958 World Cup was going to be the first with what qualified by the standards of the time as a global audience. Except perhaps for Scotland.

Television had begun to recognise the power of football to bring in large audiences – a headline in the *TV Times* trumpeted: 'ITV JOINS EUROVISION FOR THE WORLD CUP SERIES'. The football authorities had recognised it too and were determined to keep it under tight control. Up until then the only live games on domestic television had been the FA Cup Final and major internationals. The BBC and ITV were keen to expand their live portfolio beyond the big show-piece games into the League and the earlier rounds of the Cup. In the run-up to Sweden, the Football League and the FA had been meeting jointly with the broadcasters to discuss exactly that.

The talks had the tenor of a debate over the wisdom of allowing cameras into Parliament, or serious court cases. 'TV can do a certain amount of good up to a certain point. But if it goes beyond that point it can do considerable harm,' was League Secretary Alan Hardaker's gnomic note of caution. The Scottish FA President, John Park, went further, warning his own association darkly that television was a positive danger to football.

While the ruling bodies in England, Northern Ireland and Wales were acting together over World Cup television rights, Scotland had been given authority to make its own decisions. On 5 June, three days before the tournament began, the SFA announced a unilateral ban on the broadcast of midweek games from Sweden. Not just games involving Scotland, but any games. The decision had been taken at a meeting of Scottish officials at a FIFA conference in Stockholm. The junior level of the SFA – those representing the likes of Lossie juniors, clubs one step below the Highland League – said they were worried that attendances at their midweek games might suffer.

The SFA accepted their objection, and duly cabled the news to the BBC and Scottish Television. Scotland's second game, against Paraguay, was midweek; so was England's against Brazil. Given that only selected live games were being televised by the Swedes anyway, Scottish football fans faced the prospect of waiting until the semi-finals before they'd be able to see a World Cup match involving a home nation. If the television companies took any notice. It was one thing to deny their players living expenses; cabling terse instructions to broadcasters over the use they could make of their own Eurovision membership may have been beyond the SFA's jurisdiction.

My father arrived in Sweden worried that he was going to be more of a spectator than a player himself. Although he'd performed well against Poland, he'd injured his knee and was having difficulty training. Three days before their first game, against Yugoslavia, Scotland took on the local amateur team in a combined practice match and PR gesture. Although he's listed in the four-page programme, among the ads for Eskilstuna Vulkcentral tyre dealers and Old Eskil Primero ale, he wasn't fit enough to play. Nowadays, risking internationals against Sunday league players on the Thursday before the start of the World Cup would lead to trial by tabloid for the officials concerned. But in Sweden most of the teams had arranged local friendlies, and the scores had been predictably one-sided: France rattled in 14 against a town side; Yugoslavia 11; Wales knocked 19 past their hosts in Saltsjöbaden. The Scots edged past Eskilstuna 2–0.

By the time of their opening match on Sunday 8 June, my father still wasn't fit, but played anyway. Yugoslavia were a strongly fancied team, who only a month earlier had beaten England 5–0 in a World Cup warm-up game in Belgrade. A month before that England had beaten Scotland 4–0. The Scots came out of their first game with a 1–1 draw and a moral victory – it was Yugoslavia who had been hanging on at the end.

My father had been hanging on for most of the match. A challenge only a couple of minutes into the game had aggravated his knee injury. With no substitutes allowed, coming off – unless you had absolutely no choice – was looked on as letting the side down. The standard procedure for a hobbled player was to go and stand on the wing and be as much of a nuisance to the opposition as the pain would allow. Men regularly limped through matches, making up the numbers and making their injuries worse. My father at least was on the wing already. But all he seems to have done on his World Cup debut is make sure that he wouldn't be fit for the second group game against Paraguay.

The South Americans were an unknown quantity, as was most of the football world outside the British Isles. With Dawson Walker supervising the fitness work and senior players taking responsibility for tactics, that left the ten Scottish FA members in the party to look after scouting. They sent the deposed captain Tommy Docherty to watch Paraguay along with another squad player, Archie Robertson. The players returned ready to report what they'd seen to the selectors, but the invitation never came.

Fans at home were even more in the dark about Paraguay. They'd been largely unaware of my father's existence until a few months earlier; all they knew about Scotland's World Cup opponents was what they read in the sports pages. Into the Paraguay training camp on behalf of the Scottish public went the *Daily Record*'s Willie Gallagher, the doyen of the home press corps, whose pieces appeared under the byline 'Waverley – The Name that Means Football'.

I expected some of their men to be coloured but they are all white, although bearing in mind what I saw in a reservation camp in British Columbia a few years back, I would say a few of our opponents are of Indian ancestry. They do not mind the heat the least bit: indeed they are thoroughly enjoying it. They are not big men but they look wonderfully strong, broad in shoulder and big in chest. They are fast movers – over 25 or 30 yards they make the stopwatch look silly.

Waverley followed them off the training pitch into the dining room.

Most of them have never been out of Paraguay and are unaccustomed to social life as we know it. They are beef eaters and scorn fish. They have never heard of such a person as a vegetarian . . . They use no knives or forks, employing their fingers, and their adroitness, I am told, has to be seen to be believed.

They can toss a handful of mashed carrots between their wide-open lips with an accuracy of action that is almost mathematical in its precision. There are many signs that they are

ignorant of life outside their own country. But with them ignorance is bliss.

No sooner had he tucked his first dispatch into its cleft stick, than
he was sending another.

> The latest I've heard – and it seems to be true – is that they
> give way to bad temper. Some of the continental officials it
> would seem have espionages set up all over the world. They
> have been telling me that the Paraguayan players flare up so
> easily that even in practice matches among themselves they
> mix fisticuffs with their footwork on the ball!

The nation relaxed. So did the Scotland squad. While they had
drawn their opener against the strongly fancied Yugoslavia, Paraguay
had been beaten 7–3 by France.

My father watched the game from the stands along with the
Hearts inside-right, Jimmy Murray. Murray had been the hero of
the opening game, scoring Scotland's first ever World Cup goal with
a header, but he had also been injured. That hadn't stopped the
selectors from picking him for the next match. Whatever the
committee men were doing in Sweden it wasn't being done in proximity to the training ground, and their shaky grasp of team affairs
was exposed when they named the side to play Paraguay the day
before the game. The limping Murray was one of the eleven on the
team sheet; so was another hobbled player, the right-back John Hewie.

On the morning of the game the selectors were forced to announce
a new line-up, hurriedly bringing in Archic Robertson for Murray
and Alex Parker for Hewie. Celtic's Willie Fernie had already been
named in place of my father. When the team coach stopped en route
to the stadium for a meal, the selectors went into a huddle and
changed the formation from the one agreed in the morning.

Still, up in the stand my father and Jimmy Murray were confi-
dent that the team could win without them. 'I remember one guy,
the inside-left I think it was, and he was putting his hairnet on just
before the kick-off. You can imagine our reaction. But they could
make the ball speak. I was sitting there thinking, my God, perhaps
it's just as well we didn't play, y'know.'

Aberdeen's Graham Leggat, who was on the field at outside-right,
remembers the game differently: 'We thought, oh they're hopeless,
we might get one across here, but they turned out to be the toughest
team I've ever seen. They just kicked anything that moved. They
were all about 5'8" square and they just crushed us, kicked everything. It was painful.'

Whether they were outplayed or outmuscled by the South
Americans, Scotland went down 3–2 and suddenly faced a crunch
game with France to stay in the competition. The Paraguay match
had been in Norrköping, a three-hour coach journey from Scotland's
training camp at Eskilstuna, and it was the early hours of the morning
before the squad got back to the hotel. The following day the
committee had arranged for them to watch a game, Sweden versus
Hungary in Stockholm – another six-hour round trip. The players
didn't want to go. They were tired and demoralised after their unexpected defeat and they wanted to rest and regroup. First Tommy
Younger, then a whole deputation of players asked that the trip be
cancelled, but the committee wouldn't relent.

At home, the officials of the Scottish Junior FA were being
slightly more flexible. They had lifted their objections to the
Sweden–Hungary match being televised, ensuring that Scotland's
fans would be able to see the game its players were trying to
wriggle out of attending. However, they were still dead set against
the BBC showing England v Brazil because it fell on a Wednesday,
a big night for local football. In Eskilstuna, Scotland's weary squad
assembled after lunch to board the coach for Stockholm. To make

morale worse, the selectors announced they were dropping the captain, Tommy Younger.

The Liverpool goalkeeper hadn't played particularly well against Paraguay, although if he'd wanted an excuse he could have pointed to the telegram he'd received a few hours before kick-off. His wife Dorothy was being taken into hospital with heart trouble. He asked the SFA for permission to fly home to see her and to make arrangements for their two children, but the request was turned down. Dundee's Bill Brown replaced him in goal and he never played for Scotland again.

Willie Fernie had been anonymous on the left wing against Paraguay and the pressure was on for my father to return to the line-up. I can picture him, torn between the two ways he might let his country down: by not playing in the deciding group game, and by playing when he wasn't fully fit. In the end, the selectors named him in the side to face France, and this time there were no last-minute changes to the line-up.

Before the tournament began, Waverley – The Name that Means Football – had already passed judgment on the French without seeing them: 'It is generally assumed that France are a poor team and that their only worthwhile player is Kopa. It is also said that France, apart from lack of skill, are soft.' Having lost to the socially inept South Americans, Scotland knew they had to beat the effete Continentals to advance to the knockout rounds, where the national stereotypes would get tougher.

By the time they played Scotland, France had already scored nine goals, including five for Just Fontaine, who was on his way to setting a record of thirteen for a single World Cup. Still, the teams were separated by only a point. The night the Scots had lost 3–2 to Paraguay, France had gone down by the same score to Yugoslavia. A win for Scotland would guarantee joint second place in the group and a play-off, most likely a rematch with Paraguay. In the memories of most of the players, the game turned on a missed penalty by the Charlton full-back John Hewie.

Eddie Turnbull remembers it more vividly than any other incident in the competition, the details interrupting each other to tell the story: 'We got a penalty – there was no score at the time – and John Hewie steps up to take it, he was the nominated penalty taker – and he hit the junction of the upright and the crossbar and the ball rebounded – he hit the ball with such force it rebounded away – y'know how everyone lines up on the eighteen-yard line – and the ball rebounded away to midway between the eighteen-yard box and the halfway line. But France had two players up there, Kopa and Just Fontaine and and – boom-boom-boom between the two of them – instead of being one up we were one down. It was extraordinary. As a matter of fact, I had lunch last week up at the golf club with Jimmy Murray and we were talking about it. When we meet up we still talk about those games. We were really unfortunate.'

Jimmy Murray concurs with his old teammate: 'John Hewie cracked it against the crossbar and it went right away over our heads for yards, you know, and they went up and bloody scored. And that would have made a big difference. At the same time France were a great side. They had Kopa and Fontaine, they were a very good side. But we were looking pretty good for half the match and the penalty sort of knackered us. It was a distinct blow.'

It was. But the way the blow landed and the way it has since lodged in the team's collective memory are different. By the time John Hewie stepped up to the spot, Scotland were already a goal down. Just Fontaine had crossed for Raymond Kopa to score in the twenty-second minute. The penalty was awarded after half an hour, and the referee had to stop play immediately afterwards to break up a shoving match that broke out in the scramble for the rebound. France's second, from Fontaine, was a minute before half-time. There was no sucker punch, no sudden reversal. Just a missed penalty in between two French goals.

In the second half Scotland pulled one back through Rangers' Sammy Baird, but they couldn't manage another and the game finished 2–1. The players walked off the field and out of the World Cup with John Hewie's penalty miss branded onto their frontal lobes, ready to mutate into memory.

In the *Daily Record*, Willie Gallagher drew himself up to his full height, donning a new honorific like a black cap to pass judgment: 'Waverley – The World's Most Travelled, Best Informed Football Critic – points a finger at the men who made a debacle of Scotland's appearance at the World Cup in Sweden.'

John Hewie's name wasn't mentioned. Instead, the piece was a litany of Scottish FA incompetence: the failure to appoint a replacement for Matt Busby; the lack of any team tactics; the ignorance of which players were fit for selection; the fiasco of stripping the captaincy from Tommy Younger, then handing it Bobby Evans, a man who didn't want it and had actually asked to be relieved of the responsibility at Celtic. The committee were 'a bunch of amateurs'. On home ground, with a subject he knew first-hand, Gallagher's words for once had the ring of authenticity.

Back at their hotel in Eskilstuna after another long coach journey, the players had a midnight cup of tea and went to bed. Waverley's final sentence was passed on them: 'I will say with few exceptions there will be no next time for the players who brought heartbreak to Scottish football.'

In fact, there were no exceptions. By the time Scotland qualified for their next World Cup, sixteen years later, the entire 1958 squad was retired and watching on television. More immediately, though, Waverley was right in my father's case. The defeat against France was his last appearance in the national team. When the next Scotland line-up was announced in October 1958, there were only five survivors from the World Cup – including Bill Brown, who'd taken over from Tommy Younger in Sweden – and all but two of the forward line had been replaced. Over the following twelve months Scotland tried five different players at outside-left and none of them was my father. He didn't even make it into another squad. A sensational trial debut, two impressive friendlies, two ineffective, injury-hampered World Cup games – that was his international lot.

What happened? From the records, he seems to have been fit and in the Forest team around the time of Scotland's fixtures over the next couple of years. In fact, the 1958–59 season was perhaps the best of his whole career. It's another question on the long unasked list.

Even if I'd got round to asking him, though, I doubt he'd have had the answer. The trouble with trying to fathom the reason he wasn't picked is that it first requires an understanding of why he *was* picked, and the workings of the selectors were a mystery. Behind the closed doors of the committee room they could have been playing cards, holding séances, rolling up their trouser legs and trading favours to come up with a list of names.

The one man I thought might have an explanation was Ian Wheeler, whose career as a football journalist had run parallel with my father's from the very beginning. As the young sports editor of the *Northern Scot*, he'd covered St James' and Lossie juniors games. Later, based in Manchester for the *Weekly News*, he'd argued with Matt Busby over the best youth teams they'd ever seen. Per head of population, Ian Wheeler insisted, Lossiemouth's golden generation just edged out Busby's Babes.

'Why wasn't your father picked again for Scotland? Well, look at the men making the decisions. They were all on the boards of Scottish clubs. It was a time of terrible anti-English bias. I mean, take Bob McKinlay for example, who played with your dad at Nottingham Forest. He was possibly the best centre-half never to get a cap for

Scotland and he played his football down south. They would play an English-based player, but he wouldn't get that many caps – well, unless he was Denis Law or Dave Mackay.'

Unfortunately for my father, Scottish players of the quality of Law and Mackay were migrating to the English First Division in ever greater numbers. Twelve months after the World Cup there was a back-page outcry – SCOTLAND SNUB WALKER'S WONDERS! – over four of Nottingham Forest's Cup Final team being overlooked for the annual home international with England. The reason seemed to be that there were already six Anglos in the team, which was reported as the selectors' unofficial limit.

Not picking Dave Mackay simply because he'd left Hearts for Spurs would have been a national scandal. Players like my father, for whom there were home-grown alternatives – Willie Ormond, Bertie Auld, Davie Wilson – were less likely to get a chance, and almost certain not to get a second chance.

Who knows, if it hadn't been for the terrible events that prevented Matt Busby from taking over as national manager, perhaps he would have become a mainstay of the Scotland side; one of the boss's favourites, safe from the quotas and petty politics of the selection committee. Then again, if it hadn't been for that transcendent Forest–United league game in October 1957, perhaps Busby wouldn't have given him such a glowing recommendation in the first place, and he could easily have remained good company for his Forest roommate Bob McKinlay; the pair of them slipping through the cracks and down the years together into old men's arguments about the best players never to have been capped by their country.

My father flew home, disappointed that he hadn't been fit enough to do better, and travelled straight up to Lossiemouth with my mother and older brother for the consolation of the annual holiday at home. Waverley stayed behind in Stockholm as Scotland's footballing ambassador.

'WILL GERMANS TAKE ZOOM DRUG?' he shouted before the semi-final between the holders and the hosts. The piece was full of innuendo – some of it since substantiated – about how the Germans had run Hungary off the park in the 1954 World Cup Final, then promptly been sick when they got into the dressing room.

It was whispered they had been given a drug just before the kick-off. There is nothing to prevent the Germans from doctoring their players. That is something – like a lot of the weird decisions of some continental referees – for which no provisions have been made in the laws of the game.

Almost worse than the transgression itself, Waverley had divined the Germans' dark motivation: 'Like some other countries competing, they attach great value to the prestige that goes with winning the trophy.'

He turned his attention to the World Cup favourites, Brazil:

They have a psychiatrist with them. Maybe his presence is a necessity, for if there is one aspect of their make-up that could lead to their defeat, it is their hot-headedness . . . even at training today they gave ample evidence of how that can give way to excitement. There were occasions when all were shouting at the same time. Any Spanish-speaking onlooker would have been reduced to a state of utter confusion . . .

Brazil – cunningly speaking Spanish to confound the world's most travelled and best informed football critics – went on to win the first World Cup competition televised live around at least a good portion of the planet. In the process Pelé became the Greatest Player in the World, not just because of his footballing genius, but because he was able to exhibit it simultaneously to a massive and growing global audience.

Who had been the Greatest Player in the World in the 1930s? It's a trick question: the world hadn't had one, because there was no way of assembling a panel to judge the international beauty contest. In fact, a little digging usually turns up the name of Giuseppe Meazza, revered in Milan as the key player in Italy's consecutive World Cup wins of 1934 and 1938. But few of the rest of us have heard of Meazza because – in global terms – so few people ever saw him. And who knows what other, undeclared candidates there might have been, playing brilliantly in their own backwaters where the roofs of the houses had yet to see an aerial?

In 1958 television was starting to carry football across international borders without reference to parochial committee men. And fans at home could begin to test the opinions of travelling football writers against the evidence of their own eyes. I imagine my father watched the final on holiday in Scotland – that is to say I find it impossible to imagine that he didn't watch – and marvelled at the one-touch, two-syllable Brazilians. Didi, Vavá, Pelé, Goal.

Chapter Seven
Giant-killing

J ANUARY 2004. I'M FOLLOWING the 3rd Round of the FA Cup on
television and thinking about the 3rd Round of 1959.

Looking at the latest scores brings home to me how far away
from the game I've drifted. At least half of them I find impossible
to put into context; I can't tell the underdogs from the favourites.
Ipswich 2 Derby 0, is that an upset or an entirely predictable home
win in the making? Are they in the same division? Are Man City
and Leicester? Gillingham 3 Charlton 1 appears on the rolling lower-
screen caption. I know that's an upset, but how big – which division are Gillingham in?

I used to know all this stuff. For a couple of years I had run the
competition myself. From 3rd Round to Final, the whole drama was
staged in an uninterrupted marathon on my bedroom carpet, with
marbles and an upturned shoebox into which I would cut five or six
rectangular mouse holes, each with a different goal value felt-tipped
above it. Shoebox against one skirting board, me backed up against
the other, the world's greatest cup competition would begin.

I was scrupulously fair. I simply replayed key games until I got
the right result, on the grounds that I'd let the marble go before I'd
meant to, or inadvertently tried harder for one side than the other,
and therefore not been fair to (inevitably) the side I was rooting for,
secretly from myself. I never owned up to the bias – I'd installed a
mental firewall in the interests of maintaining absolute probity. In
the absence of authentic numbered balls, team names were written
on pieces of paper, folded and put into a bag. I didn't fix the draw,
trusting in the integrity of the marbles to produce the right results.

And I certainly didn't need to consult the newspaper to come up with the list of teams. I knew all ninety-two, division by division. I hadn't learned them, I just knew them, in the same way that I assumed every seven-year-old did.

These days, of course, you don't necessarily need to know. Saturday afternoon television is a social service for the context-deficient; half a dozen health visitors dropping round to the house in suits and headphones. The afternoon passes in a bantery flow of information on goals, near-goals, narks, bookings, bad decisions and diabolical liberties, Jeff; all the incident not just reported but picked apart, given a good pub going-over, well before the final whistle goes and well after it. It's addictive viewing, almost regardless of your degree of interest in the game.

The implications for Wolves of being a goal down to Kidderminster at half-time are being discussed in grave terms. Leaving aside the pedant's objection that there *are* no implications for half-time scores – no board ever sits down at the end of the season and decides to let the manager go on the basis of his appalling half-time record – I get the feeling that the upset is being willed from the studio for the sake of a decent story. Or perhaps it's more of an editorial imperative to do the 'Woe is Wolves' story now, so as to get the value out of it whether or not it actually comes to pass. Either way, the dire consequences of defeat have been thoroughly rehearsed by the time Wolves score a late goal to force a replay.

How much of a meal would be made these days of Nottingham Forest's 3rd Round tie against Tooting & Mitcham United, the only amateur club left in the 1958–59 competition? All the classic ingredients were there: the tiny ground, the frozen pitch, the butchers and bakers and candlestick-makers lining up to take on the First Division aristocrats.

Look more closely, though, and the contrasts start to fade. Any Tooting player with a decent job would have had a standard of living not very different from his professional opponent. If the club was paying him a little something disguised as expenses, he might be earning more. Press photos and pre-match television packages showing the local hero at his place of work wouldn't have cut much ice in the Forest dressing room, or with my dad's off-season workmates at the Co-op.

The game was between two sets of working men. The gulf in class between them was limited purely to football – and that was bridged by the conditions. Listening to the players' recollections of the pitch as a frozen ploughed field, I'd made the usual allowances for the slow creep of exaggeration. Then I saw the Pathé News footage, which showed an impossibly corrugated surface dusted into a giant fingerprint by snow. Billy Walker told his team that the game was off. They were just sitting down to lunch before catching the train home when news came through that they would have to play.

Now, all this would be grist to the greater drama called The Romance of the FA Cup: two or three shots of the pitch inspection . . . cutaway of the sky threatening more snow . . . word with the ref . . . quick reaction from the managers if you're lucky – if not straight into the piece to camera and back to the studio for a debate: Should It Be On or Shouldn't It? Text us now . . .

Then, Forest fans who hadn't made the journey south would have known what? More than I might have expected, it seems, thanks to Dennis Marshall, who had the BBC's radio coverage of the match played over the PA system during that afternoon's reserve game at the City Ground. 'One of the committee men said, "We'll be in trouble over this, Dennis, won't we?" and I said, "I've spoken to the FA and I've spoken to the BBC and they've both said it's OK." Well, I had spoken to them and they'd both said no. I thought, to hell with it. Now there were other games on the radio, it wasn't just Forest's – so in the gaps we used our PA announcer, who had his own way of getting results and information. At half-time he got the wind up and said, "I don't want to do this, we're going to get beat.'"

Forest were 2–0 down. A Chic Thomson clearance had hit an oncoming Tooting forward who escorted the ball into the net, then a speculative punt from all of forty-five yards had clipped the underside of the crossbar. Forest were on their way out of the Cup and on to the Sunday back pages. At home my mother was in the pantry, hiding from the radio.

'Mum, why didn't you just switch it off?' My question was actually prompted by a similar incident years later with the television. Unable to bear the tension of a penalty shoot-out during one of England's World Cup games, she'd gone and stood in the garden shed. This might have been understandable when my father was alive and she wasn't at liberty to wield the remote control. But there was only her and the cat. She claimed it was because she could still tell what was happening from the cheers and groans coming through the wall from next door. I think she needed to be as far away from the source of the torment as possible. In 1959, as a player's wife, there was no avoiding it for long.

It's inevitably the non-playing partners in a relationship who suffer the most, sitting helpless in the stands, marked out from the rest of the crowd by their special agenda of anxiety. My mother was always a nervous spectator, unable to really enjoy any games involving my father as a player or as a coach: 'I get too het up.'

He played, she worried. Later on, we all played and she worried. Outnumbered four-to-one in her own home, my mother was the family repository of worry. It wasn't just the fear of my father getting hurt or dropped or sacked – although that was always there – it was everything else she had to think about while he concentrated on football.

'I don't worry about things I can't do anything about,' he would say to news of her latest concerns over money, or us children, and sink into a deep and immediate sleep. Yet he kicked her through every night of their married life. Something was going on while he was unconscious, and it manifested itself as a game: a replay of Saturday's just gone, or a rehearsal for this Saturday's coming. Perhaps it was his way of dealing with the forces he could do nothing about. Perhaps he just dreamed at dog level, chasing through-balls every night instead of rabbits.

I don't know how long my mother spent in the pantry, but Forest came back in the second half to scrape a draw. One of Tooting's frozen ruts betrayed them, diverting a back pass away from the keeper and into the net, then the referee gave a penalty for something only he had seen. 2–2. The replay at the City Ground kicked off pessimistically early to allow for extra time, but on a level playing field that could take a stud Forest won 3–0, with my father scoring the third.

It's become a cliché, a staple of every team's successful cup run: the early-round scare, the game they should have lost that – in retrospect – becomes a turning point. But we no longer have the patience for retrospection. In 1959, FA Cup upsets either happened or they didn't. Now, there's too much money invested in the game for everyone concerned not to extract maximum value. So the giant-killing story is told in advance, as a hedge against it not being supported by the facts once the game begins. That way we can all enjoy The Romance of the FA Cup before reality arrives to reclaim the plot. Of course, once all the narrative machinery of press, radio and television has been brought to bear on the build-up, anything less than the storyboarded outcome can only be a letdown. But in the FA Cup the letdown is the massive ante-post statistical favourite.

The chief giant-kill in prospect for the 2004 3rd Round is Liverpool at the hands of Yeovil Town. Proud traditions are evoked, precedents are cited from 1949, and the whole business of extrapolation begins. A good thirty minutes before kick-off Liverpool have lost, Gerard Houllier has been sacked and the big question is where does this proud club go from here and who'll be the man to take over. At half-time they're a goal up and cruising. In the tunnel, the reporter is under instruction not to give up the ghost of giant-killings past. He ropes in the Yeovil manager for a quick séance before the second half: 'There's a touch of mist – just as there was in 1949 . . .'

Forest's close 3rd Round shave happened and was then reported. Our attention span won't allow games just to happen now; they have to be nudged into one of a handful of narrative shapes set aside for the purpose. The stories are standing by, waiting for the facts to coincide: 'And if that had gone in it would have been the quickest World Cup goal . . .' 'If Roy Keane had scored in his Sixth FA Cup Final it would have been a great story – although Andy Marshall is a good story himself . . .'

Of course, the game has always been full of stories, brimming over with them. We don't watch just to marvel at cold technique. But now the stories are driving the game, or at least the way we're invited to think about it. Half the old pros I talk to say they watch with the sound turned down.

Forest went on to beat Grimsby, Birmingham, the cup-holders Bolton Wanderers and Aston Villa – the magnitude of their 3rd Round escape at Tooting & Mitcham growing quietly in the rearview mirror round by round.

Chapter Eight
Players' Pool

IN APRIL 1959, SHORTLY after Forest beat Aston Villa in the semi-final, Billy Walker was the guest speaker at a meeting of Nottingham businessmen. On the verge of his second FA Cup Final as a manager – an astonishing twenty-four years after the first with Sheffield Wednesday – he'd been invited to talk about the secrets of successful man-management, perhaps, or his own professional longevity.

But he had most to say about the Players' Union portrayal of its members as slaves. His players were better dressed than he was – indeed, better dressed than the committee men who ran the club. Sixteen of them had cars. 'A fortnight ago,' he told the assembled businessmen, 'the majority of our "slaves" picked up £38 in one wage packet.'

That quote gave the *Daily Express* its headline: 'FOREST SLAVES GO BY CAR TO PICK UP £38'. I think Billy Walker may have underplayed his indignation by a pound. The previous season the maximum wage had gone up to £20 a week – although not year-round as the players had been expecting – and the win bonus to £4. Two days after beating Villa, Forest had put five past Preston North End away in a league game. On top of the wage and the win bonus, a cup semi-final was worth £15, making a grand total of £39.

In any event, it was an interesting choice of subject matter for a manager whose side was weeks away from its biggest ever game. His examples of player affluence were telling too. Nice suits? Cars? These were things that he and the club's committee men had enjoyed for years and took for granted. His wages were double theirs.

Billy Walker wasn't accusing the players of wealth beyond the dreams of avarice, just beyond their station. Elsewhere in the same paper, an FA Council member was objecting to England players travelling in first-class railway carriages where the officials sat. And Mel Charles, brother of John, was being vilified for using an agent to try to negotiate his transfer from Swansea. The Football League President, Joe Richards, called it 'a sickening business', and promised that the agent would not be recognised by any clubs.

There was no public response from the Forest players to Billy Walker's outburst. They hardly needed to justify their earnings under the League's mandated wage scale. And anyway, they understood the real reason for his irritation. After the semi-final win, the manager had taken his players away for a few days to a hotel in Blackpool. He'd called a meeting and offered to act as their agent for any commercial opportunities that might come their way as cup finalists. The players had turned him down.

'I mean, Billy Walker was the kind of guy, he'd ask you for half-a-crown for the porter when we were going on the train to away games. And the first two or three times you'd actually fall for this. Then you'd be chasing him for the money back, for your half-a-crown.' As one of only two players in the side with a medal of any sort at senior level, Chic Thomson's opinion carried a lot of weight, but the No vote seems to have been unanimous.

'Well, he was a likeable crook,' Johnny Quigley, the Glaswegian inside-right told me, 'a likeable rogue, but he wouldna gi' you too much, man.'

The players set up their own pool. They posed in their kit with the dray horses of the local brewery – 'The Two Popular Favourites' – they opened fêtes, they held a Forest players' dance. Jeff Whitefoot, who'd had big-club experience at Manchester United, was in charge of going out and looking for business. Jack Burkitt signed the cheques along with Chic who was treasurer.

'I remember the pre-cup final dance. Jeff Whitefoot was taking tickets at the front door and flogging them at the back door – incredible. But we didn't make much. The likes of United and these people, they would be making tons more, but it was a battle with Mr Walker because he wasn't getting his pennies.'

If the players had needed justification for their decision to earn themselves some extra cash, the sports pages were full of it. Nine days after their semi-final defeat by Forest, Aston Villa announced that they were sacking sixteen players. Half their squad would be made redundant at the end of the season – without the benefit of redundancy money. A cup final appearance might have saved Villa's season and a few players' jobs.

The following day there was more serious news. My father and his teammates were to undergo tests for polio, along with half a dozen other teams who'd played Birmingham City in the previous six weeks. Birmingham's England international right-back, Jeff Hall, was seriously ill in hospital. There was talk of the Easter fixtures being postponed. My father had lined up against Hall three times in nine days: a pair of 5th Round draws and a 5–0 Forest rout in the second replay.

The tests were all negative. But the brevity and fragility of an athlete's career was made frighteningly real. Polio was rare; broken legs and torn ligaments happened weekly. Jeff Hall died two weeks after being admitted to hospital.

Nobody now can remember how much money the players' pool generated. Whatever the sum, Billy Walker had been denied his agent's commission. On 16 April, with less than three weeks to go until the final, the manager called his players together for another meeting, and afterwards issued a public statement: 'All fundraising activities are suspended from now on. We've got to get down to football and nothing else before the final. Soccer is no longer going to be a sideline. They are tired from all their outside commitments – it has got to stop.' It was true that Forest had suffered a drop in form, but no one inside the club believed that was the sole reason for the ban.

In the papers, the players were being cast as a bunch of spivs. The reason had nothing to do with fundraising dances or adverts for the local brewery. It was because they were selling their tickets.

Profiteering from the trade in scarce commodities had sharp and unpleasant associations for working-class football fans who'd suffered through shortages that had persisted well beyond the war. Less than five years earlier, when my father had signed for Derby, he'd shared front-page headline space with the news that butter was off the ration for the first time in fourteen years. No doubt many supporters thought the team had earned the right to make extra cash out of their achievement in reaching Wembley, maybe they'd even bought tickets to the Forest players' dance. Tickets to the match, though, were a much more emotional subject.

Wembley famously held 100,000. By the time the FA had taken care of the great and the good, the blazered and bewhiskered, the two finalists received 15,000 tickets each. Just over half of these were distributed among the 72,000 Forest fans who applied for them, via a bizarre display of public transparency by the club. 'Yesterday three anonymous blind men drew from a 75-gallon red-painted barrel the letters of about 8,000 fortunate fans . . . ' began the report in the *Evening Post*. That left 64,000 or so ticketless members of the Nottingham public to compete for the remainder with corporate hospitality firms, travel agents and the usual assortment of sheepskin-coat wearers. For all of them the chief source of tickets was the club, and soon stories began circulating about the team's own distribution system.

Each player got a dozen or so tickets – half of them seated, half standing – with the option to buy more. In with their allocation was a slip of paper from the FA warning that all the serial numbers were on record. But players selling their comps was a football tradition. After Forest's 5th Round tie at Birmingham two City players, Trevor Smith and Dick Neal, had been accused of personally hawking their tickets outside the ground before the match. Once they were in the Final players didn't need to leave the house. Fans knew where they lived because they lived alongside them, and plagued their doorsteps like carol singers out of season.

The Forest players used to congregate in a café near Trent Bridge after training; Notts County players used a slightly scruffier one on the other side of London Road. In the weeks before the Cup Final a few of the Forest squad seem to have crossed the street to County's café to talk to the owner, Bob Green, who was buying and selling tickets in large quantities. The fall guy in the story varied depending on who was telling it – it was Peter Watson, the reserve centre-half; it was Tommy Wilson, the centre-forward; it was Wilson acting for half the team – but the name of the villain didn't. Bob Green took delivery of an unspecified number of cup final tickets from a Forest player who naively agreed to call back later for the money.

Dennis Marshall is certain it was Tommy Wilson: 'Tommy went at the agreed time and when he got there the woman behind the counter said, "Oh, he's just gone out – he said could you leave the tickets and he'll give you the money when he gets back." Tommy said OK and he left the tickets and went and fed the bloody swans on the Trent. When he went back, not only had the café owner and the woman gone, but it was all boarded up and they never did see him again. And the police never found them either.'

Bob Green had been making copy in the national press for weeks. He was openly advertising tickets in the café window and selling them over the counter. It was the usual grubby tout's tale – and now it included Forest players. Once the police were called in, at the insistence of the club secretary, Noel Watson, there had been no keeping the story quiet. As late as the day of the Final itself, the *Daily Express* caricatured the Forest team as a group of briefcase-carrying businessmen.

My father hadn't been involved in the café fiasco but he did make a profit on his tickets. After he'd taken care of family and friends, his allocation went to Jack Watson, a local builder who'd done jobs on the house. He kept one ticket for himself, sold the rest and the pair of them split the proceeds.

Lower down the food chain, some of the Forest staff were doing the same. The committee magnanimously gave almost everyone associated with the club not only Cup Final tickets, but return rail packages to ensure they could afford to make the trip. In the week after the final, the club's travel agent received a spate of refund requests from employees who'd been 'unable to go' for one reason or another. They'd sold their tickets, but the travel vouchers were in their names.

Chapter Nine

Watching the Cup Final on Television

UNBELIEVABLY, ALMOST UNFORGIVABLY, I'D never watched the 1959 FA Cup Final.

I'd seen the goals countless times, especially the first: my father shrugging off the Luton Town full-back and cutting a perfect ball into the path of Roy Dwight. But I hadn't seen the whole thing – we didn't have a tape. Sometime in the 1970s my dad had tried to get one, writing to Bob Wilson who was then presenting the BBC's *Football Focus*. He'd sent us some highlights – twenty minutes' worth – which apparently was all they had.

The suspicion remained that there must be something more substantial in the archives, and when my father became seriously ill I'd thought about going back to ask again. But apart from one brief exchange in the hospital when he was first admitted – 'I think I'm finished, don't tell Mum' – we'd never acknowledged that he was dying, and to flash his life before him on videotape seemed somehow an affront to his stoicism.

So it was only afterwards that I called the BBC. I knew people who knew people and I wasn't expecting it to be much of a problem. But word came back that Bob Wilson had been right the first time – all they had in the library was a highlights edit and shots of the homecoming parade through the streets of Nottingham. When I'd gone searching for my father's appearance on the very first *Quiz Ball* – broadcast live from St Joseph's Hall, Highgate in 1966 – I had been prepared for failure from the start. A football-themed quiz show that might never get off the ground was hardly likely to head the BBC's archive priorities. But the 1959 FA Cup Final? How could they not have the 1959 FA Cup Final? My father's finest hour wasn't a wedding speech captured on Super 8 and liable to be lost in a house move, it was the broadcast record of the nation's greatest sporting institution.

'Yeah I know, I'm sorry, but we just don't have it. I was really surprised myself.' The *Match of the Day* librarian couldn't have been more sympathetic, but the '59 Cup Final seemed to have joined *Dixon of Dock Green* and early episodes of *Dad's Army* among the ranks of the BBC's disappeared.

And that's where I would have left it had it not been for Dave Pacey, the man who scored Luton's only goal in the final. I'd called him up to talk about his memories of the goal and the game, when he let slip that he had the whole thing on tape – he'd got it from the BBC eighteen years earlier. This raised twin prospects: either the match was still crouching in the dark somewhere deep inside the BBC, invisible to the filing system because of a computer glitch, some cataloguing mistake; or – much worse than never having been kept at the time – it had been wiped only in the past couple of decades.

I went back to my man at the BBC, who agreed to look again. He called me a couple of weeks later with some news: he'd located three uncatalogued rolls of film in the system which might be the Final. He wouldn't know for certain until he'd ordered them up from the vaults and threaded them onto a machine. The VHS arrived a month later.

There's no preamble to the game, just a black-and-white clock. Film was too expensive to waste on preserving 'Abide With Me' and the teams walking out of the tunnel. The tape starts with a shot of the centre circle; the referee is checking his watch and three Luton players are standing round the ball waiting to kick off, each figure inside his own sooty aura of film grain. The camera pulls back slightly and there's my father at the bottom of the screen with his back to me, shifting his weight from one foot to the other and rubbing his hands in anticipation.

Kenneth Wolstenholme, the voice of all our football yesterdays whether we ever heard him commentate live or not, tells us that this is the seventy-eighth FA Cup Final, the thirty-first at Wembley. The game starts. He indicates the flow of play simply, naming the players as they assume and release possession: '*Whitefoot, Gray, Imlach* . . .' The story of the match tells itself.

'Whitefoot, Gray, Imlach' is the prelude to Forest's opening goal after nine and a half minutes. It's a five-man move, with my father the only player to touch the ball more than once between the Forest half of the pitch and the back of the Luton net. A long kick by the Luton goalkeeper is headed infield from the left-back position by Joe McDonald. At seven o'clock on the centre circle Jeff Whitefoot pivots through the ball on the bounce, sending a casual-looking half-volley towards the left-wing. It's actually a perfectly weighted pass but the Forest inside-left Billy Gray can't resist the urge to tamper with it, jumping to add a little momentum with his head. The ball, which was on its way to my father's feet, is now heading outside him towards the line.

His first touch is the one that makes everything which follows possible. It's a neat flick executed on the turn, using the weight of the incoming pass to redirect the ball – and himself – past his marker, Brendan McNally. Wrong-footed and realising he's beaten, McNally reaches out to grab his opponent's shirt, but my father shakes him off, and within two or three strides he's got yards on the Luton right-back. The speed of the man is breathtaking. As he cuts in and heads for the box, the director panics and cuts too: tight on him haring towards the dead-ball line for no more than a second, then back again to the wide shot.

Steady in the control room now, don't lose your composure and ruin the only moving pictures of my father's finest moments.

As he enters the lower left-hand corner of the penalty area there's a flick of the head to see what his options are. *'Wilson's in the middle . . . '* suggests Kenneth Wolstenholme. But my father has seen beyond him. Five defenders including McNally have tracked back into the area. Without breaking stride, he cuts them all out of the action with a tighter than right-angled ball back towards the edge of the box. As it clears the penalty spot Roy Dwight arrives to strike it first time.

The ball hits the net and the goal slips untouched into the past. Unmediated, self-contained, perfect. It nestles into the memory, bedding in for posterity.

Every goal we see on television now is remembered for us – immediately, serially, externally – before we get the chance to remember it for ourselves. Before we can register the experience of the singular unrepeatable moment, it's already been repeated six times from four angles, so that what actually gets remembered is a seventh-generation copy – a fatally corrupted file, contaminated by analysis and diluted with all kinds of information that wasn't in the original.

Instinctively, my right hand pats the sofa beside me for the remote control, then I check myself and let the handshakes happen and the game restart in its own time. There's no replay.

Five minutes later my father swaps roles with his inside-forward, feeding Billy Gray out on the flank with a right-footed pass. Gray dummies inside, steps back and lofts an open invitation to the far post, where Tommy Wilson rises unchallenged to put a no-nonsense working man's forehead to the ball. It all has the smoothness of inevitability. The Forest players are relaxed, they've been here before. Billy Walker brought them to Wembley during the week to walk on the pitch and practise climbing the steps to the Royal Box to get their medals.

Up in the stand the wives sit together, sharing the worry. For once, their picture will be in the papers too – hatted and handbagged and captioned without first names of their own. It's Mrs Roy Dwight whose worst fears will materialise today.

They've already suffered a sort of trial by social ordeal. Their husbands left Nottingham early and enjoyed a relaxing week in Hendon: they went to Lord's to watch the cricket; they played, rather than trained, on a local park near the hotel, putting down tracksuit tops for goals like schoolboys. A few of the committee men joined in and the players took great pleasure in putting them on their backsides. Billy Walker took the odd corner.

The wives had to face the Savoy on their own. Plates of asparagus were set in front of them like straightened question marks to which they had no answer. The cutlery was a silver-plated trap set to go off if they dismantled it out of sequence. Waiters hell-bent on humiliating them sprinkled cheese on their soup.

But after the game's first quarter of an hour, even the most nervous among them has allowed herself the luxury of exhaling and starting to enjoy the spectacle. From her seat my mother can make out the polka dots on the Queen's hat, below and to the left in the Royal Box. Further below, the Forest men are already two goals up and treating Luton the way they had the committee members on the park at Hendon.

One committee man has made his own small contribution to their mood. Half an hour before kick-off Frank Chambers appeared in the dressing room. By this stage the players were each in their individual bubbles of concentration, performing the solo routines that would help them come together and perform as a team. Billy Gray was having a cold shower, Joe McDonald was smoking in the toilet, Bob McKinlay was waiting, making sure that everybody else had started to change before he began himself. My father had already cracked his pre-match egg into a glass of sherry and downed it in one, for stamina.

This close to the game a suit, unless it belonged to the manager, was an unwelcome sight. Thirty seconds of awkward bonhomie and a couple of well-meaning platitudes to endure before getting back to the business at hand. But Frank Chambers had a ritual of his own to perform. He went round the players handing each one a gift – a pair of see-through frilly knickers for their other halves, specially made at his lingerie factory in Forest colours, a lace rosette on one side.

'He produces these things just as we're getting ready,' says Chic Thomson. 'It was madness, but it just broke all the tension anybody might have felt. I've never seen players so relaxed and I've played in some big games. Y'know, pointing in the crowd saying, "Look, there's so-and-so." And the way we started was absolutely wonderful, the football was tremendous. If Roy Dwight had stayed on the field we'd have made five or six, without any doubt.'

On the tape, as on the field, the collision looks nothing special. It's almost a minute later that my father kicks the ball out of play to allow Tommy Graham on with the magic sponge. He waggles Dwight's right ankle and flexes the knee. He doesn't know the leg's broken. Neither does Dwight. While the camera checks on the injured Luton man he gets up to stamp his weight on it, and has collapsed again by the time we cut back.

'*No substitutes, of course, allowed – this is a competitive match,*' Wolstenholme reminds us.

Subs are for friendlies. None is allowed in the league or the cup and won't be for another half-dozen years. Remarkably, Forest have fielded the same eleven players from the 3rd Round to the Final. By the time the St John ambulancemen have performed their pall-bearers' walk with the stretcher, it's looking as though they'll have to play the last sixty minutes with ten.

The unluckiest man in the stadium isn't Roy Dwight, though. It's Geoff Thomas. Dwight has a fractured shinbone, but he also has a goal and he's going to get a winner's medal. Thomas, a one-club player with fifteen years' service at Forest, has been twelfth man for every round of the Cup. Now that injury has finally struck, all he's called on to do is ride shotgun in the ambulance.

At Wembley Hospital half a dozen or so male patients are gathered in their dressing gowns on a semicircle of chairs around the television set in Barham Ward. Suddenly, as though John Wayne had climbed off his horse and into the room from the afternoon feature film, the Cup Final turns from small-screen black and white to life-sized and somewhat surreal colour, as they're asked to make way for the scorer of Forest's first goal. Roy Dwight, minus his boots but otherwise still in his full kit, is lifted into a bed with a cage to keep the blankets off his right leg, and settles in to watch the second half.

'It was sad when he went off because we were playing well' – this is Johnny Quigley – 'but second half your old man played out of his brains. It was hard playing with ten men at Wembley because it takes all the stamina out of you. You thought you were getting sucked under the ground. But your old man was going like a bomb, he had a tremendous game that day, tremendous. He was the best man on the park.'

'Stewart played everywhere' – Chic Thomson now – 'Billy Gray sort of came back and played behind the other three, but Stewart was playing left-half, left-wing, centre-forward, outside-right. In fact, Bobby Mac says to me, "He's going to keel over." He never stopped, just tremendous.'

I've been primed with these rave reviews of my dad's performance long before sitting down with the tape. It's hard not to feel a little like a critic measuring a film against impossibly rapturous advance word of mouth. But then I'm armed with all sorts of information that makes this a different match to watch now than it was to watch then, let alone to play in.

I get special satisfaction when he steals the ball from Luton's Billy

Bingham – the same Billy Bingham who will sack him as first-team coach at Everton twenty-seven years later. A sort of pre-emptive revenge, but only for me. There's a twinge of sympathy for a diving header that goes just wide from Bingham's teammate Allan Brown – together he and my father will lead Blackpool to within a point of promotion, before they both get the push.

Luton pull a goal back. In the stand my mother has nowhere to hide, except behind her hands. Along the row, Pat Thomson looks down at hers and realises they've destroyed her hat. Her husband throws himself at a swinging boot to smother an equaliser and needs treatment. Geoff Thomas is on his way back from the hospital, he'll miss everything except the presentation.

'*No doubt there are going to be quite a few critics eating their words at twenty minutes to five . . .*' says Kenneth Wolstenholme. This is the first Cup Final for a decade without a team from the game's northern heartland. Plenty of columnists have written it off in advance.

The film reel changes. Chic Thomson jumps back in time during the overlap, lining up to take a goal kick twice.

'*Imlach, right back with his own defence . . .*'

My father's putting in a tackle by the corner flag. Billy Gray's ahead of him, socks rolled down, suffering cramp. The pitch looks perfect, but players from both sides have already told me how much of it is sand. Now he's in the centre circle, picking up the ball just inside his own half. He's at the edge of the Luton box before he has to check stride; he hasn't beaten anybody, he's just outrun them. There's no Forest player to cross to.

'*Well, he's got to do this on his own . . . goal kick to Luton Town with eleven minutes to play . . .*'

As the goalkeeper runs to retrieve the ball, the Luton left-back is doubled over from the chase, his hands on his thighs as he tries to recover his breath. My father walks past him, jaw flexing.

Of course, he's not winning the game single-handedly – I'm

watching it single-mindedly, choosing moments. If I were Bob McKinlay's son – or Jack Burkitt's or Johnny Quigley's or Chic Thomson's – I could choose others. But he's giving everything. And as the pitch and the pressure start to tell on the players of both teams, he seems, as he did in those charity games I remember as a child, to be playing at a different speed from everybody else.

'*Morton a little slow and it's Imlach . . .*'

In the ninetieth minute he steals the ball off the toe of the Luton centre-forward at the halfway line, and he's close enough to shoot before anyone closes him down. After ninety-two he wins the ball on the right from a goal kick, runs it out of play, and wins it back again from the Luton throw-in.

'*Up to three minutes of injury time now . . . this must be heartbreaking for Luton Town supporters. And for Nottingham Forest supporters enough to bring on a heart attack . . .*'

He's still running after the final whistle. As a gaggle of Forest players fall into each other's arms in the centre circle, he's just visible racing through the bottom corner of the shot on his way back towards his own goal and – I imagine – his best friend, Bob McKinlay.

In the main stand a dozen or so well-dressed women are in tears. At Wembley Hospital the staff are still waiting to treat Roy Dwight. Only once he's seen Jack Burkitt lift the cup and accept two medals from the Queen will he allow them to wheel him away for X-rays. He's thinking about the midweek walk-through, grateful to Billy Walker for giving him a mental template of the view from the Royal Box, which he can match up with the scenes on television. But before they can collect their medals, the players have to pick up their teeth.

'A lot of us had teeth missing,' says Chic Thomson, 'four or five of us, including your dad. And we were deciding what to do with 'em because somebody had said, "You can't meet the Queen without your teeth." And of course we didn't play in them, we usually left them in the dressing room. Somebody said, "We'll put them in Charlie's cap." I said, "No, what happens if someone belts one in and they're all mashed up, it'll be worse."

'So in the end Tommy Graham had a big red handkerchief, like the kind of thing you'd put on the end of a pole if you were leaving home, and we put our teeth in there. Nobody noticed it, but at the end of the game Tommy had the hanky out and he was saying, "Come on, get your teeth," and I'm saying, "Well, they're not mine, y'know." It was great.'

Chic got his. My father's stayed in the red handkerchief, forgotten in the excitement. The Queen would just have to deal with it. You can see the gap in his smile as the players fight their way off the field through the ranks of the Royal Marine Band, marching out of the tunnel in the opposite direction for the post-match ceremonials. His jaw is still flexing, as though the mechanism takes a few minutes to wind down once he's stopped running, and his arm keeps shooting up into the air to acknowledge someone he sees, or thinks he sees, in the stand.

When the Forest players get to the foot of the steps something strange happens. It's as though they have a collective flashback to years of pre-season punishment running up and down the stands; they all break into a sort of decorous jog and mount the steps to the Royal Box like dressage horses. There's half a suspicion that they'll launch into a sequence of star jumps in front of a baffled monarch when they reach the top.

I'm familiar with the medal ceremony from the highlights tape we've had at home for years, so mentally I've all but switched off by this point, certain that I've seen anything new that there is to see from the '59 Cup Final. Then I'm ambushed by a moment I'm sure my father wouldn't have remembered and wouldn't have recounted if he had. Halfway up the steps he breaks ranks, bends to pick up a dropped rosette and hands it to one of the fans leaning over from their seats to clap the players on the back. It may not be a rosette, it's hard to see, but it's white and the fans lining the steps are all Luton supporters, wearing straw boaters in support of the Hatters.

This time I can't help but reach for the remote control. If I had to pick an image from the ninety-odd minutes of the afternoon preserved by the BBC, I'd settle for that one: my father, minus false teeth, jogging up the steps of the Royal Box towards the Queen and the pinnacle of his career, then stopping to pick up something dropped by a fan – a fan of the other team most likely – and handing it back to him.

On television, his medal moment takes place behind the classic Cup Final shot of the victorious skipper holding aloft the trophy. When he comes into view, not yet past the last dignitary in the receiving line, he's already opening the small leather present the Queen has given him. '*It's all right*,' says Kenneth Wolstenholme, '*it's in there, Stewart*.'

Chapter Ten
Man on a Train

IT MUST BE A newspaper picture. A free print from one of the photographers who covered the team, when free prints were all that was needed to keep the press–player relationship harmonious. I'd like to know who took it, but the copyright stamp has faded now and the photo itself doesn't seem to have made it past the picture desk, at least not into any of the papers I've searched.

The post-cup final editions had been full of the usual stuff: the captain with the cup; his teammates jigging on the Wembley turf with the accessories (as third in line up the steps to get his medal it always seemed to me as a child that my father had won the lid). A couple of days later there were the aerial shots of the homecoming crowd, the team smiling and waving at them from an open-top bus. The departures from the standard template showed Roy Dwight surrounded by his teammates in hospital, or being wheeled off the coach to huge cheers.

But this is a shot worth its space on any inside page. It could be a movie still. Down the wood-panelled corridor of an old-fashioned rail carriage, my father is walking towards the camera like a perfect scale model of Cary Grant. He shows no signs of the previous night's celebrations. His Forest cup final suit is immaculate, his tie is unloosened, his cigar echoes the angle of his splay-footed gait, and he's looking straight out of the frame into the future as he carries a tea tray back to the dining car.

The shot was probably posed – behind him you can just see a reporter leaning against a compartment door, his notebook partly shielding his face – but it doesn't matter. It captures my father at the high point of his career and perhaps his life. The dazed joy of the post-match pictures from Wembley has been replaced by a kind of assured aura. The readers' poll in the *Daily Herald* had declared him Man of the Match. Stan Matthews, the boyhood hero he'd queued to watch in a wartime exhibition game, had declared him Man of the Match. On the front page of the *Sunday Express*. A week later he'd be on the same train heading south again to pick up his award at a gala dinner in London.

He's twenty-seven. He looks like a man walking into the rest of his life (via the dining car) with supreme confidence. Of course, he doesn't know what I know looking back at him. That in a year's time he'll be sold to the team he's just helped to defeat, Luton. That by then they will have been relegated to the Second Division. That a change of manager will see him sold on within months to 3rd Division Coventry City. That chance and circumstance will send him click-clacking down the league like a wooden acrobat in a Victorian child's toy. A figure which looks secure enough at the top, but only needs a gentle nudge to send it tumbling with unstoppable momentum.

'I OFTEN WONDER WHAT WAS in Billy Walker's mind after the Cup Final because that team was broken up so quickly it was unbelievable . . .'

Chic Thomson sits across the room from me and shakes his head. I've heard the same thing from other members of Forest's '59 side. I haven't heard what he's about to say next though. 'The biggest surprise was sitting in the Savoy Hotel on the Monday morning after the match. Bob McKinlay, your dad and myself went to have a cup of tea. And Billy Walker came in and spoke to your dad and said, "Stewart, I want you to go to Sheffield United." And he walked away then – that's all he said – Bob and I, our mouths were down here, your dad didn't say anything. Then we all looked at each other and said the man's crazy. Your dad had just got the Man of the Match award, he ran his guts out. I couldn't believe it. We sort of laughed about it, but within about twelve months Tommy Wilson, your dad, Roy Dwight didn't play – didn't really come back from the broken leg – Joe McDonald, myself all sort of taken off the . . .' His sentence peters out like the team did.

This man has the sharpest and most comprehensive memory of anyone my father played with in his whole career. Perhaps it's something to do with being a goalkeeper: the solitary, watchful presence at one end of the field – the pitch spread out in front of him wider than it is long. The goalkeeper is a kind of super spectator, with a heightened perception and a telescoped view, knowing that he might be called on to join in at a second's notice.

There's no one with whom I can check Chic's memory of that

incident at the Savoy; he's the only one of the four men who were there still living. If the plan to sell my father to Sheffield United was a serious one, it never came to anything. Forest's more immediate priority was to cash in on the team's collective worth with a post-season exhibition tour of Portugal and Spain.

In Spain the team played four games in seven days, three of them in the last four. To avoid the heat they kicked off at 10 p.m. in Valencia and had to be at the airport at 7.00 the next morning. In his hotel room at 2.15 a.m. – the time is underlined at the top of the postcard – my father writes home that the team will go straight to bed when they reach Madrid for a couple of hours' sleep before playing Athletico. They got thrashed 6–1. Athletico fielded a handful of guest players including Barcelona's brilliant Hungarian, Ladislav Kubala. The crowd was lower than expected due to bad weather – only 45,000 instead of the 75,000 who'd turned out in Valencia – but it was still lucrative business for Forest.

The final game, in Cadiz, hadn't been on the original tour itinerary. The players were tired, but Cadiz were a Second Division outfit; one last easy opponent and then they could get home and bask in the afterglow of the FA Cup win. Cadiz, though, was just the venue. It turned out that Billy Walker had committed to a match against Athletic Bilbao, who'd just won their own domestic cup competition. Instead of a day's souvenir shopping for their wives and children before heading home, the exhausted Forest team found themselves on another plane south for a game being sold to the public as a serious contest for Anglo-Spanish bragging rights.

They protested, but the tickets had already gone on sale. A handful of Forest players cried off with injuries and Bilbao won comfortably, 3–0. It was an unnecessarily sour note on which to end the tour. As the party gathered at the airport for the flight home, Chic remembers Billy Walker approaching my father with a package that he wanted carrying through customs for him. He waved away questions about what might be in it, but once his back was turned a small group of players gathered round my dad to open it, and found it stuffed with pesetas.

'Now we always made sure when we went abroad that we got so much a game and if we won there was a bonus and they paid for our laundry – and he used to fight that, Billy Walker, it was terrible trying to get the money off him. But this was an extra game and we weren't being paid for it – he'd said, "Oh no, it's all, y'know, gratis." And we said, "What's Stewart got in his bag?" And eventually he gave us a little bit of it each, but he was a terrible man that way.'

When my father got home there was a club-crested envelope waiting for him. Nominally from the man who'd just asked him to carry foreign currency through customs, it was his contract offer for the following season.

29th May 1959

S. Imlach Esq.

In accordance with the rules of the Football Association and Football League we now have pleasure in advising you of the terms for the 1959/60 season which we are prepared to offer you when your present contract runs out on the 30th June 1959:

1st team	Reserves	Summer
£20	£15	£15

As we mention, the present agreement ends on 30th of June and your acceptance (or non-acceptance) of the terms offered to you must be in my hands at least seven days before then. Failure to return the forms enclosed properly signed where marked (or non-acceptance) will result in your getting no wages from this club after that date.

Sign the forms, in ink, in all those spaces marked 'X' before returning. By the way, details of the date for the commencement of training for the 1959/60 season will be posted to you around the end of June so make sure that we have the appropriate address to which we can send this notice.

Yours sincerely,
W.H. Walker,
Manager

I've got the letter in front of me. The club apparently hadn't got round to ordering new stationery, or was thriftily working its way through existing supplies, because the letterhead bears the singular legend 'English Cup Winners 1897–8' alongside the quaintly informative 'Colours – Red Shirts, White Knickers' and above both the Club Secretary's and Manager's home telephone numbers.

It's a pro forma covering letter, the same one all the players would have received. It's impossible to take offence at its tone because it has no tone, it's just a piece of business correspondence. But still my skin prickles with indignation reading it because, even allowing for the restrictive template of 1950s etiquette, it exposes the true nature of the relationship between club and player. Beneath the camaraderie and club spirit, the gung-ho team talks and appeals for loyalty, the committee men in the dressing room slapping backs and handing out frillies for the wives, here's the real relationship: master and serf.

'Terms we are prepared to offer . . . must be in my hands . . . non-acceptance will result in your getting no wages . . .' Couldn't they at least go through the motions? Make some nod towards the great emotional tribal dance that had just taken place. Some acknowledgment of the glorious effort these men had put forth in red shirts

On the train home to Nottingham
after the Cup Final.

One of my father's two goals in a 7–0 Forest win against Burnley in 1957.

Doncaster Rovers' goal-keeper Harry Gregg dives at my father's feet. The future host of *The Golden Shot*, centre-half Charlie Williams, looks on, 1956.

A packed City Ground during Forest's promotion season of 1956–57.

Me, my mother and older brother Steve waving my father off for the benefit of the local paper, Coventry, 1961.

The Imlach jaw-flex, Crystal Palace, 1965.

Thirteen minutes into his Crystal Palace debut, 18 August 1962.

The only booking of my father's career, for haranguing referee Pat Partridge after an Everton defeat at Derby in 1973.

(*Above and right*) Taking training at Bellefield.

In discussion with Everton manager Harry Catterick and fellow coach Tommy Casey.

Everton with the League Championship trophy, pre-season, 1970.

The trophy comes to Glenmarsh Way.

(*Above left*) The 1958 cap, made in 2000 by Brian and Janet Turner of Majestic Trophies in Nottingham.

(*Above right*) My father's FA Cup-winner's medal.

(*Left*) Reproduction Scotland cap, genuine Scottish pride.

and white knickers. Couldn't they just recognise in passing that this addressee in particular had run himself into the ground and been singled out for his part in football's annual showpiece game? Of course not, and it's hopeless naivety to think otherwise.

In any event, I don't imagine that my father bothered reading the body of the letter; the formalities wouldn't have changed from one season to the next. What mattered were the figures and these evidently hadn't been to his liking. He was scarcely out of the first team during his time at Forest, yet whenever he was, even if it was through injury, his wages dropped by 25 per cent. In the off-season it was the same.

After a three-season run which had brought promotion, First Division consolidation and Forest's first cup win of the century, my father might have expected to be offered the best of the bad deal that was available to him. But £20, £15 and £15 was the opposite, pretty much the least the club could plausibly offer. Anything more than a £5 drop from the basic wage would have been getting insultingly close to the legal minimum of £8 a week. Over the previous twelve months he had been arguably Forest's best player, yet the club wasn't even offering him the maximum off-season wage of £17. Whether he'd asked around in the dressing room, or whether his dissatisfaction at the offer was entirely self-generated, he turned it down.

I know this because there's an undated second contract offer preserved in the same envelope as the first; identical covering letter, different figures. On this one his summer retainer has been increased to £17 and his reserve-team wages to the same amount. For the reserves, though, the red typewritten £17 has been altered to £20 in blue Biro, with Dennis Marshall's signature next to it. Finally, and for what I believe is the only time in his career, my father was going to be paid the maximum wage available to a professional footballer.

★ ★ ★

His first season as a fully remunerated Forest player was a poor one. It started in August 1959 with defeat in the Charity Shield by Wolverhampton Wanderers and ended one spot above the relegation placings. With Roy Dwight's recovery from his broken leg taking longer than expected, my father spent the first two months of the season on the right wing. Along with a couple of injuries of his own, he also hit the first sustained loss of form in his career and found himself dropped. When Forest faced Reading as FA Cup holders in the 3rd round on 9 January 1960, Johnny Quigley was the only surviving member of the Wembley forward line from eight months earlier. My father finished with thirty-one appearances, not bad but still his lowest in five seasons with Forest. His insistence on getting the maximum, in or out of the first team, paid off in a dozen of his wage packets.

There was no haggling come contract time at the end of the 1959–60 season. When the retained list was published Bill Whare, right-back in the Cup Final team, wasn't on it. He was one of seven players released, with another two put on the transfer list. Only twenty-four players were retained compared with thirty-three the season before, but that wasn't what made the headlines.

'FOREST TO PAY PLAYERS BY RESULTS' was the back-page lead in the Nottingham *Evening Post* the week after their final game. One bad season in five had given the upper hand back to Billy Walker and he was hitting out with it: 'At Forest we pay good money. We have a right to expect a good return for our money. This new scheme means players in the first team will receive £20 a week – the maximum we are allowed to pay at the moment. If a player falls into the reserves then he does not deserve top money and we shall pay him £17 a week.'

Billy Walker was hardly going out on a managerial limb; Arsenal had done the same thing the previous season, guaranteeing top money to only five of their international-packed team. But he didn't stop at wage cuts. He also curtailed players' rights to earn money outside the game. Those with part-time winter jobs had to give them up before the club would re-sign them. With his Wall's Ice Cream signs and his joinery work, my father was facing a drop in income on and off the field.

What I found remarkable about this story is how little story there was. Having read the initial piece in the *Evening Post* of 17 May, I had settled in to my seat at Colindale for a week's worth of bitter back-page wrangling. But there was nothing. No row, no repercussions, no follow-ups at all in the days after the announcement. The original article had carried a single quote from an unnamed first-team player: 'It seems a little hard that after good years we have a wage cut as soon as we run into a bad patch.' That was it. If there was any serious fallout from the decision to cut players' wages it was kept within the club, thanks partly to the relationship between the management and the local press.

As in Bury and Derby, the team beat writer on the *Football Post* in Nottingham operated under a pen name. And as in Bury and Derby the price for access was acting as a largely unmediated conduit for the views of the club. The *Evening Post* writers did have real names, but they were no more hard-hitting.

National papers were keener to exploit footballers as personalities, and less reliant on the goodwill of a local team. Post-game quotes were still a rarity in the nationals, but features and player columns had started to appear. They were uncontroversial, by and large, but they were enough to rattle the Football League. At consecutive AGMs in 1958 and 1959 the League Management Committee had discussed a McCarthyesque-sounding proposal to outlaw 'journalistic activities' by players. In the end they had delegated the power to clubs, which in most cases amounted to the same thing.

Two weeks after the wage-cut announcement, the *Post*'s back page carried the starkest possible confirmation that the paper enjoyed a closer relationship with the club than its employees did:

IMLACH MAY GO TO LUTON

Terms have been agreed between the clubs for the transfer of Stewart Imlach, Nottingham Forest's Scottish international outside-left, to Luton Town. Imlach is to be contacted today . . .

Imlach is to be contacted today? So the Nottingham *Evening Post* was officially informed about the deal before my father. Surely the first he heard of it can't have been when he picked up the paper? 'No, I think Den came round to tell him,' said my mother. 'The club certainly didn't say anything to him.'

'Your dad was astounded,' Dennis told me. 'They used to do a lot of that, football clubs did. You really were a chattel to be bartered. The two clubs would have agreed – even to the extent of what date they were going and how much money the player would get at Luton as distinct to Forest. Some just threw up their arms – your dad probably did – and said, "Oh well, bugger them if they don't want me."'

The suddenness with which my father disappeared from Nottingham's sporting radar I found quite shocking, like having a favourite character in a serial abruptly killed off with no satisfactory explanation. The first story breaking the news of his transfer was the only one in the *Evening Post*. It ran on a Monday, there was nothing on Tuesday and by Wednesday the fans' attention was already being directed elsewhere: 'REDS MOVE QUICKLY TO SIGN ARSENAL ATTACKER LEN JULIANS.'

So that was it. No debate about the wisdom of the deal, no look back at his Forest career, no statement from the manager thanking Imlach for his services and wishing him well at his new club, no farewell or fanfare in the papers. Perhaps it was because I knew what came next that I was hoping for some kind of public valediction.

Three days after he dipped below the surface of Nottingham's newsprint, my father bobbed up in Luton's. The *Luton News*, 'Every Thursday' – a bad sign, his career was slipping back from daily into weekly instalments. The *News*'s chief football correspondent wrote under the name Chiltern and spelled my father's name Stuart. The back pages that preceded his transfer were full of bad omens: the team had just been relegated from the First Division; it had no manager; the directors had misgivings about signing any players until a new man was in place; anyway, reports from the team's pre-season foreign tour suggested their search for a left-winger had been solved from within – their own Mike Tracey was playing superbly.

How dare they sign him – gamble with his career – when they could see the potential problems themselves. The Luton players were shocked, not that their board should want to buy the man who'd tormented them in the Cup Final, but that Forest had been willing to let him go.

'I just couldn't believe it, I couldn't understand it. I personally thought what the hell's Stewart done to warrant that, y'know.' Ken Hawkes was Luton's left-back in the Cup Final, but he'd been keeping half an eye on my father's career for years. He thinks the directors were belatedly making amends for a mistake they'd made in 1952. Ken had been in digs at that time with another Luton player, Wally Shanks, brother of Willie Shanks, the scout who'd recommended my father to Bury. 'Luton could have had him two or three months before he went to Bury. Dally Duncan, the old Scottish international, was manager and Willie recommended Stewart to Dally Duncan. Nothing materialised and the next we heard of him he was playing for Bury. Of course it left a bad taste in the mouth when Stewart was in the Cup Final because he could have been playing for us.'

Although the move had been presented, as moves routinely were, as a fait accompli, the *Luton News* reported a slight hitch when the chairman, P.G. Mitchell, met his latest acquisition: the player wanted his wife to see the accommodation on offer before he signed.

His wife, the wife. Just as club chairmen were too important to have first names, wives weren't important enough. These days, players would be put up in a hotel or rented accommodation while the lengthy business of house-hunting went on. Then, the whole fraught procedure was reduced to a multiple-choice question at the end of an afternoon's drive around an unfamiliar town – pick one from four. Rather like those bookclub subscription offers, with a list of uninspiring introductory titles from which you go through the motions of selecting one because that's all there is on offer; the difference being that you had to live in your choice.

Luton, when my father joined them, were an ageing team with low morale. The arrival of Sam Bartram as manager a month before the season started doesn't seem to have improved the mood. Bartram had been Charlton Athletic's goalkeeper for twenty-two years and was widely considered unlucky never to have been capped for England. In his first managerial job he'd taken York City from the Fourth Division up into the Third.

'Poor old Sam's dead now. He was a very good goalkeeper but . . .' Ken Hawkes trailed off diplomatically. Albert McCann, the Luton inside-left, didn't: 'He was thick. When you were a kid at school you always stuck the dummy in goal, didn't you? I'm being unkind because there are some very intelligent goalkeepers, but he wasn't one of them.'

In his first interview after taking over he made it clear where he thought the strength of the team lay: 'In Bingham and Imlach we have what I consider to be as good a pair of club wingers as there is in the country and if the three men inside can grasp the opportunities they are bound to create I can see goals coming.' By the end of October both of them had been sold, Bingham to First Division Everton, my father to Third Division Coventry. Faced with a group of veteran players sceptical of his managerial ability, Bartram had apparently decided to dismantle the team and start again.

'He came in with the idea of cracking the whip and he just scuttled about eight players at the same time,' said Ken Hawkes, who was one of them. Albert McCann fell out with Bartram and left too. The 1960–61 season was barely eight weeks old when my father signed for Coventry, and he had yet to make ten appearances in a Luton shirt. He'd gone from the First Division to the Third in the span of a dozen matches.

Click-clack.

Until this point I'd never really grasped the timescale of my dad's career in its later stages. The list of his clubs had always had a natural rise and fall to it: Bury, Derby, Nottingham Forest – pause for a beat – Luton, Coventry, Crystal Palace. Nine syllables up, nine down. I knew the sequence of steps to and from the high-altitude plateau in the middle of his career, but I didn't know the tempo. Discovering the abruptness of his decline was like coming across an old spool of cine film in the attic that showed him falling silently and inexplicably downstairs.

The Coventry *Evening Telegraph* report of his signing sounds as puzzled as I am reading it that City had managed to land a player with First Division soil still on his boots. It dwells on his FA Cup and World Cup credentials, it shakes its head over the speed of his tumble down the divisions – 'Thus the Scot will have played First, Second and Third Division football in the space of about two playing months!' The paper's account of the transfer itself (the *Telegraph*'s boardroom confidant wrote under the name of Nemo) adds personal detail to what would have been a routine piece of horse-trading for the time.

The deal took place in a Chester hotel where Luton were staying after playing Liverpool in a midweek League Cup tie. Coventry's manager, Billy Frith, had watched the game in order to give my father the final once-over. The club chairman, Derrick Robins – freshly installed on the promise of money for new signings – had driven straight to the hotel to oversee the negotiations. One of a new breed of forward-thinking club chairmen prepared to release their Christian names to the press, Robins sat with Frith and Luton's P.G. Mitchell to thrash out the details. Only once a deal had been struck was the merchandise produced. According to the report, my father was roused from his bed around 1 a.m. to be informed that he had been sold.

I can picture the scene: fresh brandies ordered despite the hotel bar being officially closed, cigars newly lit to celebrate, Derrick and Percy perhaps on first-name terms now: *'Well, I think we have a deal, gentlemen, shall we get him up?'* Once again my father asked for time to discuss the prospective move with his nameless wife, although Nemo seemed to think this a formality. Woken in the early hours of a Thursday morning, he had signed by six in the evening and was in the Coventry side that Saturday. His first meeting with his new teammates would be in the dressing room at Highfield Road before the match.

If the sheer speed of the move had distracted my father temporarily from reflecting on his plunge down football's lift shaft, his debut must have brought it home to him. Coventry's opponents were Bury. His first club had been relegated from the Second Division the same year he'd won promotion with Nottingham Forest. Now he was back down at their level – lower in fact, because Bury came to Highfield Road as Third Division leaders, while Coventry were closer to the bottom of the table than they were to the top.

His debut ended in a 2–1 defeat which left City a point above the relegation places. Christ, he could have ended up in the Fourth Division, setting some sort of record: the man who played at all four levels of the professional game in the shortest space of time. Of course, I could read ahead and reassure myself that this wasn't going to happen, but he couldn't.

Then again, it was me getting upset about it. Where he played was one of the things my father couldn't control and refused to worry about. As far as I can tell, he slept soundly and looked forward to Saturdays.

Chapter Twelve
The End of the Maximum Wage

MY FATHER HAD GONE to Third Division Coventry because he was sent. They had bought him because they could afford to.

There was no mystery to it. The retain-and-transfer system lay across the league like a deadening fog. And players responded by limiting their own horizons too, as a pre-emptive strike against disappointment. The fact that most of them still felt a sense of privilege that they were paid to play football at all obviously helped.

Tom Finney — as in so much else — was the classic example. Back in 1952, three years before Eddie Firmani signed for Sampdoria and five before John Charles's famous move to Juventus, the Preston North End and England winger had been approached during a tour of Italy. The president of Palermo offered him a two-year deal: a £10,000 signing-on fee, wages of £130 a week, bonuses of up to another £100, a villa in the Mediterranean, a car and free travel between England and Italy for his family.

Finney agreed to put the offer, which included a £30,000 transfer fee, to his club. The minutes of the next Preston North End board meeting preserve their official reply:

> The chairman reported that T. Finney had approached him regarding an offer received from an Italian club for his services. Unanimously agreed that the player be informed that we could not accede to this request. This player had been retained with the FA and was expected to re-sign for season 1952–53 on his return from holiday.

Finney's biography records his own stoic response:

> To be quite honest I didn't expect North End to react any other
> way so I accepted the decision without too much fuss and decided
> the best thing to do was to try and put the whole business out
> of my mind . . . perhaps I was lucky in some respects that the
> decision wasn't mine to take.

Finney had been thirty when the Preston board blocked his move
to Italy. He was thirty-eight when he retired at the end of the
1959–60 season, just as my father was being shipped off to Luton
and the Players' Union – by now the Professional Footballers'
Association – was drawing up the list of formal demands that would
lead to the abolition of the maximum wage. In the intervening eight
seasons his total earnings from Preston North End added up to less
than the signing bonus he'd been offered by Palermo.

Also around the same time that Forest were selling my father,
George Eastham was being denied a move to Arsenal by his club,
Newcastle. In a league where transfer requests were routinely turned
down this would have been nothing out of the ordinary except that,
unlike Tom Finney, my father and countless others up and down the
country, Eastham didn't shrug his shoulders and decide he'd better
make the best of it.

He appealed to the Football League to step in and arbitrate, but
as far as the League was concerned it was strictly a matter between
player and club. Eastham sat down for talks with his manager, Charlie
Mitten. Irony must have hung like cigar smoke over their discus-
sions in the office at St James' Park, because Mitten was only ten
years removed from the greatest contract-breaking scandal in English
football history, the Bogotá Affair.

Charlie Mitten was the left-winger in Manchester United's first
great post-war side, and like every other man in the League he'd

been slack-jawed to see two Stoke City players, George Mountford and Neil Franklin, sign hugely lucrative deals to play in Colombia in 1950. On a US tour with United that summer he took a call from Franklin in his room at the team hotel in New York. Franklin passed the phone to Luis Robledo, the millionaire owner of Santa Fe in Bogotá, who made him the same offer he'd made the other two: £5,000 to sign and £5,000 a year. There was a plane ticket waiting for him at reception the following morning.

When he broke the news to Matt Busby, his manager forbade him to go. But the difference between Charlie Mitten and Tom Finney two years later – apart from Finney's heroic decency and sense of loyalty to Preston – was that Mitten didn't need the permission of his club. England's retain-and-transfer system was effectively part of a worldwide cartel, because no country affiliated to FIFA, the game's governing body, would help a player break the terms of another member country's contract system. But the Colombian league was operating outside FIFA's jurisdiction and its two big clubs, Santa Fe and Millonarios, were racing each other to build multinational superteams.

In the event, their imports were limited largely to malcontents from England and from Argentina, where there had been player unrest in 1949. Santa Fe and Millonarios had the likes of Alfredo Di Stéfano and Héctor Rial in their line-ups long before Santiago Bernabeu won European Cups with them at Real Madrid. At this remove Luis Robledo looks like a thoroughly twenty-first-century team owner, but his grand scheme and Charlie Mitten's career in South America came to an end when Colombia was readmitted to FIFA. On his return to England Mitten was fined £250, suspended for six months, then sold by Manchester United to Fulham. After four years there he moved into management.

So in 1960, fully rehabilitated and part of the football establish-ment, Mitten found himself sitting across the table from his younger, less cavalier self in George Eastham, while he tried to muster the conviction to play Matt Busby. Whatever might have passed between them in the privacy of the manager's office, Newcastle as a club was adamant that Eastham should stay. If he refused to sign a new contract he would get no wages, and since the club retained his registration there was nowhere else he could legally play within the professional game. It was the same hopeless battle that players had been fighting and losing for decades.

A Newcastle director boasted that he'd see Eastham shovel coal rather than let him leave the club. But Eastham did leave. He walked out in the summer of 1960 once his contract had expired, took a job as a salesman with a friend who ran a business in Surrey and waited. His quiet, dignified determination matched the eminent reasonableness of his case. As far back as 1947 the future Conservative Cabinet minister Walter Monckton QC had called the Football League terms of employment 'The worst contract I've ever seen'. League Secretary Alan Hardaker – the man employed by the clubs to defend the system – agreed, although he could only say so years later in his autobiography: 'They were fighting to keep a system of retaining players that was not only ludicrous but which, very clearly, would not stand up in law.'

The problem for the Union had been finding a player on whose behalf to fight a test case. Mitten himself could have fitted the bill on his return from Colombia, but had decided instead to do his time and get back into the English game as quickly as possible. A few years later there was the Aldershot right-back Ralph Banks, who was being retained by his club without pay. But before the case reached court Aldershot neatly sidestepped proceedings by releasing him on a free transfer. In the slight, skilful, unassuming Eastham, the PFA finally had the perfect candidate for a challenge to the retain-and-transfer system.

★   ★   ★

The edifice of English football was under a two-pronged attack from the forces of change as the 1960–61 season began. While the workers were massing at the back door shouting for the removal of the contractual leg-irons they'd been wearing since the turn of the century, television was on the front step with a chequebook. Both the BBC and ITV had made offers to televise live matches: ITV to the League for a featured game of the week, the BBC for a package of FA Cup games.

With hindsight it looks like perfect timing, an opportunity to strike a deal with one in order to finance an agreement with the other. In fact, most club chairmen viewed television as scarcely less of a threat to their continued prosperity than the PFA. The '50s have been filed in the collective memory as football's heyday: black-and-white photos of Lowry paintings, with gapless terraces of endlessly repeating hatted heads, and the occasional locked-out stick figure climbing over the fence. The truth was that crowds had been falling from their post-war peak for most of the decade, and club chairmen thought television could only accelerate the decline. P.G. Mitchell at Luton was typical: 'Why should we help breed a generation of armchair viewers for the game?'

Before the start of the 1960–61 season the FA had an offer on the table from the BBC of around £45,000 for six live cup ties. ITV was prepared to pay closer to £150,000 for twenty-six league games. Their proposal entailed delaying the kick-off of their chosen match until 6.50 on a Saturday evening. Coverage would start at 7.30, allowing ITV to catch the last few minutes of the first half, sell some advertising during half-time, then show the rest of the game without interruption. More importantly, they were prepared to guarantee the gate money.

Alan Hardaker and the Football League's president, Joe Richards, agreed the deal, and on 10 September 1960 Blackpool's home game with Bolton became the first live league match on British television.

The Big Game was to share the 7.30 slot with *Saturday Spectacular* for the rest of the season. This was football as prime-time entertainment. Billy Wright, the former Wolves and England Captain who'd already crossed over by marrying one of the Beverley Sisters, was signed up to do colour commentary.

But the first *Big Game* was a flop. For one thing the main box-office draw, Stan Matthews, was injured and didn't play. And ITV put their cameras high up behind the goal at Bloomfield Road rather than on the halfway line in the main stand. The critics complained that the commentators overpraised what everyone could see was a poor game, and talked about a packed house when the crowd was only 17,000 in a ground that held more than twice that many.

The next live fixture on ITV's schedule was Newcastle's visit to Arsenal the following week. After Bolton's dour 1–0 away win at Blackpool this was a spectacular 5–1 rout by the home side. But it was seen only by those who'd paid to go through the turnstiles at Highbury. ITV viewers got the *Nat King Cole Show* instead – Arsenal's board had refused entry to the cameras. Spurs and Aston Villa, whose match was next on the list, declared their opposition too, and as Everton, West Bromwich, Wolves and Birmingham lined up behind them it quickly became clear that Hardaker and Richards had made a pact without the authority of their club chairmen. The deal collapsed, ITV withdrew their offer, and in the fallout from the whole affair the BBC did the same with their proposal to show FA Cup games.

There's no way of knowing how great the pace of change might have been then, or how different the game might look now, but the great reshaping of football by television that took place in the 1990s could have begun three decades earlier; in fact did begin, only to be suffocated in the boardrooms of the old First Division.

If the Football League hadn't had other pressing matters to deal with, perhaps the live-television experiment could have been revived. But by November 1960, the PFA had called in the Ministry of Labour to try to get a response from the League to their proposals over pay and contracts. For the next three months the men who ran the game would be distracted by the threat of a players' strike. The union had a package of demands, but the key elements were the ones the clubs were most adamant they wouldn't concede: the abolition of the maximum wage and the end of retain-and-transfer.

For the clubs, the television issue had been clear-cut – they were in a position simply to say no to it. Many of them believed they still had a similar prerogative over the wishes of their players. Decades of turning them down flat had cemented in the minds of chairmen their right to continue doing the same, even as it became increasingly clear that the PFA, under its new chairman, Jimmy Hill, was cultivating an air of militancy among footballers more widespread than had ever been managed by his predecessors. Despite Newcastle caving in and transferring George Eastham to Arsenal in late November, the union persuaded him to continue his legal action against the club in order to challenge the retain-and-transfer system in court. And all around the country dressing-room doors were being closed on players-only meetings to gauge the appetite for industrial action.

At Luton, P.G. Mitchell refused to accept the vote in favour of a strike and demanded that it be restaged in front of him. 'They had all the players into the boardroom,' Brendan McNally told me, 'and he says, "I want a show of hands of the players who are not going to accept a maximum wage" – and all the hands went up except three. He was trying to put the squeeze on us, see who'd put their hand up and then they'd have their eye on you.'

Ken Hawkes's was one of the hands that went up in defiance of his chairman. 'He said, "I hope you know what you're doing, you're going to be out of a job." And Allan Brown, the union rep – Al was a pretty forthright guy – he says, "Are you trying to frighten me, Mr Mitchell?" He says, "No, but it just won't happen, you're fighting a lost cause," and he did everything to convince us that it was silly.'

After the votes at club level a series of mass meetings was called. At the first, in London, southern players came out overwhelmingly in favour of a strike. In Coventry, the City chairman, Derrick Robins, tried to stop the Midlands vote going the same way: 'I gather the impression that the majority of players at yesterday's meeting didn't want to strike but were swayed by one man. It may suit that one man to have a strike but the vast majority of footballers know that a strike is not in the best interests of themselves or their clubs.'

The one man Robins was referring to was Jimmy Hill, whose ability to unify players in pursuit of a goal must have impressed the Coventry chairman as much as it alarmed him. Within a year he'd be offering Hill the manager's job at Highfield Road. In Birmingham, as in London and Manchester, the vote was for industrial action.

In the meantime, the antique machinery of the game continued to wheeze and rattle. In the week before Christmas 1960 Stan Matthews was reprimanded for playing in a charity match. He'd appeared with his son, a tennis player, in a fundraising Tennis Stars v Showbiz XI game. This was in breach of Football Association Rule 18a banning players 'under the jurisdiction of the FA playing with or against unaffiliated clubs'. An FA official reported that Matthews had given a written undertaking not to do it again.

The threatened strike is popularly remembered as being about the abolition of the maximum wage, partly because it's an easier headline, partly because in the end that was the only objective it achieved that wasn't fudged afterwards by the Football League. But the maximum wage was actually conceded comfortably in advance of the planned strike date.

Backed into a corner by the first week of January 1961, League negotiators had finally agreed with the PFA not only to remove the maximum, but also to bring in a new system of arbitration to safeguard a player's rights at the end of his contract period with a club. Chairmen were due to vote on the deal on 9 January. But the concession on contracts generated so much hostility from the clubs in advance of the meeting that it was never put to a vote. The negotiated changes were simply deleted. Instead, a vote was passed in favour of a unilaterally altered deal which covered only the lifting of the maximum wage. The retain-and-transfer system was clearly more important to clubs than keeping a ceiling on earnings. And the chairmen calculated that they could buy the players off with one in order to keep the other.

It didn't work. A new series of mass meetings was called starting on Wednesday 11 January, spread over three days so that the union leadership could address each one. Fresh mandates for strike action were issued region by region. My father was one of only two Coventry players who accompanied their PFA delegate, Ron Hewitt, to the Midlands meeting in Birmingham. Not that I really felt the need for proof of which way his vote had been cast: I may not have known him as well as I should have, but I knew him this well.

Birmingham City's delegate, Brian Farmer, spoke outside the hall afterwards: 'We were prepared to accept these proposals until we realised that the transfer clause was still in its original form. This must prove to the public that we are fighting for principle – not money.' At their meeting the next day the northern players let in the press to prove that they weren't being mesmerised by Jimmy Hill.

With the strike set for Saturday 21 January, the League tried to squeeze one last game's worth of revenue out of the players. Telegrams were sent to every club in the country telling them that the entire

fixture list was being brought forward to Friday night, or Friday afternoon for clubs without floodlights. Any players who refused to appear
would be considered in breach of contract. The PFA discussed coun-
teracting the move by bringing forward the start of the strike. The
pools companies hedged their bets and printed two coupons, one
featuring the usual slate of English and Scottish League games, the
other Scottish games only – split into half-time and full-time scores.

It was a stand-off. No more talks were scheduled, the only
exchanges were in the press: the League promised that games would
go on as normal using replacement players; the TUC called on its
members to boycott blackleg matches; the PFA talked about staging
its own league on Hackney Marshes or in Ireland; there was muttering
about players in club houses being evicted.

Even when the Ministry of Labour brokered last-ditch talks on
the Wednesday before the strike was due to start, Joe Richards gave
no grounds for optimism: 'I will be at the meeting if my presence
means avoiding a strike but I am not going to waste my time. I am
not budging on the transfer system, which must remain as long as
there is a league competition in this country.'

By Thursday the 19th, he had agreed to a whole raft of changes.
No transfers could take place during the term of a contract except
by mutual consent of player and club. And if the two couldn't agree
on a new contract at the end of a season there was a detailed and
transparent series of steps to protect the player's earnings and his
rights. It wasn't the contractual free-for-all of club chairmen's night-
mares, but it was the end of the feudal system under which the
players had laboured for so long.

The strike was off, the weekend's fixtures were back on and the
papers all reported the result the same way: LEAGUE END SOCCER
SLAVERY . . . HILL'S HOUR OF TRIUMPH . . . HE LEADS PLAYERS TO VICTORY
AND FREEDOM.

But that's not the way history remembers it, and the reason is simple: the clubs reneged on the agreement. Just like the Football League's live-television deal with ITV, this one lasted as long as it took for the chairmen to meet and vote it down. At the decisive talks, presided over by the Minister of Labour, John Hare, the League contingent had insisted that they had a mandate to negotiate the necessary changes. Afterwards, an extraordinary general meeting was called for April, and the clubs they represented refused to ratify the key element in the package. Joe Richards talked as though 19 January had never happened: 'Come what may we intend to keep the retain-and-transfer system.'

Speaking in the House of Commons, John Hare was as unequivocal in his support for the union as a Conservative Cabinet minister could be. The players were right and the League had been informed of the government's view. MPs from both sides of the chamber put down a motion calling for the original agreement to be ratified. The League and the PFA peddled their conflicting versions in the press. There was a pre-Clintonian debate about the meaning of the phrase 'deal with the matter' in the wording of the pact.

By this time it was almost the end of the season. There wasn't much leverage in a summer strike. Anyway, the original momentum for one was now bogged down in a messy argument over interpretation. The retain-and-transfer system lurched on like Rasputin under a hail of claims and counterclaims.

It would be another two years before Justice Wilberforce got in what looked like a clean shot to the head. In his 1963 judgment on the long-delayed George Eastham case he called it 'an unreasonable restraint of trade . . . Indeed to anyone not hardened to the acceptance of the practice it would seem inhuman and incongruous to the spirit of a national sport.' Even then the League found room for manoeuvre in the subordinate clauses of a 16,000-word judgment, and the system, although vastly improved, wouldn't finally die until the Bosman ruling three decades later.

Incredibly, the clubs also tried to stymie the part of the package they had ratified – the abolition of the maximum wage. Shortly after the deal that had averted strike action, club chairmen met at the Café Royal in London, where they tried to agree a new unofficial maximum among themselves and behind the back of the League. Their plans were sabotaged by one of their own: Tommy Trinder, the comedian and chairman of Fulham. Trinder, who presumably had an appreciation of the market value of entertainers, had told the press he'd happily pay the England captain Johnny Haynes £100 a week, if only he could. Now he could and – happily or not – he did.

But Haynes was the exception not the rule, even at his own club. My father's Scotland teammate Graham Leggat was in the line of players waiting behind Haynes to be called into Trinder's office: he came out with a £5-a-week increase. At Coventry, and at most clubs around the League, the wage increases were more Leggat than Haynes. My mother never saw her husband's pay packet, but she doesn't remember much of a change in her housekeeping money.

Still, this was the fork in the road for the players and the people who watched them. Footballers were finally going to be paid what they were worth, which inevitably would be more than the ordinary working fans on the terraces. It was the beginning of the end of the local neighbourhood football star, the man who lived and socialised in the community where he played.

Not immediately, though, and not for my father. Coventry finished the 1960–61 season strongly, with a run of results that might have earned them promotion if only they hadn't started it from just above the relegation zone. While his teammates dispersed for the summer, my father was down at the ground five days a week. He'd signed on as a joiner with a company that had a contract with the club to do refurbishment work, and spent the off-season building a new direc- tors' entrance at Highfield Road.

Chapter Thirteen
A Telephone Conversation
with Jimmy Hill

TEN MONTHS AFTER HE'D stood in a packed hall in Birmingham listening to Jimmy Hill as a union leader and fellow player, my father sat in the dressing room at Highfield Road and heard his first team talk as a manager.

In November 1961 Coventry sacked Billy Frith and his three coaches after they went out of the FA Cup to the part-timers of King's Lynn. That was the trigger, but Frith was obviously due the bullet anyway, because the chairman already had Jimmy Hill lined up as his successor and named him the same day. Hill's first public statement on taking over was a slightly shaky declaration that, as a union man, he was very unhappy about the four sackings.

A week into the job, he lifted Coventry's ten-year-old ban on players talking to the press. The next day, the League Secretary Alan Hardaker was talking to the press himself, publicly drawing Hill's attention to Rule 76, which made permission contingent on the understanding that the player would not bring his club or the League into disrepute. He followed it up with a letter to the Coventry directors, reminding them of their responsibilities and asking them whether they supported their new manager's decision.

It doesn't seem to have started a feeding frenzy at the dressing-room door. The first post-match player quote in the *Evening Telegraph* wasn't until four months after Hill's announcement. It's this bombshell – attributed to my father but in words sounding very like the reporter's – on how he took advantage of a defensive mistake to make the second of Coventry's goals in a 3–2 defeat at Bristol City: 'Briggs tried to trap the ball before sending it back to his goalkeeper but he did not control it properly and I took it before he recovered.' Alan Hardaker could sleep easy.

My father was playing well and had been pretty much since he signed, so it was a surprise when he was suddenly dropped in April 1962, towards the end of Hill's first season in charge. The manager went out of his way to emphasise that he wasn't simply being rested: 'You don't rest a man in the reserves.' It sounded like some kind of bust-up, especially from Hill's pointed remark, but it seems to have lasted no more than a game.

The following week my father was back in the first team – and for a few glorious seconds, back at Wembley. With Crystal Palace standing in for Luton and the quagmire of Highfield Road momentarily smooth and green, he beat his man, looked up and cut a perfect ball back for the incoming Roy Dwight to score with a first-time shot. Dwight had never properly recovered from his broken leg in the Cup Final, and he'd been out of the League for a year. Jimmy Hill remembered him from their early years together at Fulham, and had signed him from Gravesend & Northfleet where he'd been playing part-time.

The reunion lasted only half a season though. I skipped the last few match reports in the *Evening Telegraph*, looking for the story I knew was coming.

CITY TRANSFER STEWART IMLACH — BUY LAVERICK
Saturday 30 June 1962
. . . they bought Bobby Laverick, a 24-year-old left-winger from Brighton, and transferred outside-left Stewart Imlach to Crystal Palace. Jimmy Hill described both fees as 'reasonable' and added: 'but we came out on the right side'.

The transfer of Imlach comes as a surprise for he was one

of City's leading forwards last season playing in all but one of their games and scoring 7 goals.

At last, a living manager. Jimmy Hill was the seventh of my father's career, and the first who was still around to tell me why he got rid of him. Just as importantly, he was forthright enough not to dress his reasons up for the sake of tact. Still, I didn't dive straight in when I telephoned him. We covered his union days, his anger at the Football League for reneging on the 1961 deal, his reasons for going into management, and the various innovations he'd tried at Coventry. All interesting stuff, forcefully reminisced.

Then: 'So, Jimmy, as a player you'd have known my father before you got to Coventry, you'd have come up against him with Fulham . . .'

'Oh yes, I was well aware of him. Outside-left is a position that the game is still short of players you can rely on – they're always in short supply, more these days it seems than in the past which is surprising – but I'd had Bobby Laverick who I'd bought for £2,600 from Everton [Brighton, actually, Jim – but I wasn't going to interrupt his flow of memory now we were onto the subject matter that mattered]. He played one game and I said, "Thank you very much, Bobby, you can go and find yourself another club," and I had to look round suddenly to find people to fill that hole as it were . . . and Stewart was . . . a left-footed player . . . and just as the game . . .'

No sooner is he onto the subject of my father than he's off again, generalising about why the game has become short of left-sided players, being Jimmy Hill. And he seems to have my dad's departure and Laverick's arrival the wrong way round. After a respectful pause I tried steering him back.

'Now you sold my father and bought Bobby Laverick on the same day.'

'Yeeeah . . .' It's the first syllable he's uttered with anything less than full Hillian conviction, long and drawn-out, buying himself time to cast around in his memory. 'Yeah . . . when you say I sold him . . . I can't remember selling him. Had he not gone when I arrived? We were short of a left-sided player which is why I signed Bobby Laverick, and I didn't get rid of anybody.'

Bloody hell, he's forgotten him. I'm well-used to the unreliability of memory by now: the erroneous certainties, the unpredictable gaps, the random fog of Alzheimer's. I've become acutely aware of how poor my own memory is for events much closer in time to me than most of the ones I'm asking others to dredge up. But this is something new: a man with what seems like a reasonably robust memory except for a hole in it the exact shape of my father.

'Yeah, at the end of the 1961–62 season you sold my dad to Palace and bought Bobby Laverick on the same day.'

Astonished silence.

'Well, at the end of the '61–62 season . . . I thought I'd signed Bobby Laverick before my first season. I'm just thinking, when I went to Coventry what time of the year was it?' I fished out my photocopies and transcripts from Colindale to make sure. 'Wednesday 29 November, so you took over halfway through that season.' Then I read him the story of the simultaneous departure and arrival of my father and Bobby Laverick, complete with the quotes he gave to the *Evening Telegraph*.

'Does that ring a bell?'

'Well, it does. The fact that it wasn't in my memory . . . how old was your dad at that time?'

'Just turned thirty.'

'Yeah . . . that's amazing, so I would have seen him that season. In fact, in my mind the Coventry team that starts to take shape is the one with Bobby Laverick at outside-left. As I say, he played one game, it might have been two or three, then he was out of the side and I bought Ronnie Rees.' He's right about that. The records show a grand total of four games for Bobby Laverick in a Coventry City shirt.

'It was like an instant decision. He was a well-built lad, a six-footer and well-muscled but he just didn't use any of those attributes to help the team win. And that's so funny because Stewart would have been there from November onwards . . . it's a sort of blank. I can't evaluate how that came about. Certainly I'd have rather had a 35-year-old Stewart than I would have had a Bobby Laverick.'

Whether that was tact or the truth didn't really matter. The greater and unavoidably insulting fact was that Jimmy Hill had managed my father for half a season – picked him, played him, dropped him, sold him – and had no memory of doing any of it. He didn't even remember him as the other half of his first big transfer market mistake, an episode which had at least ensured that Bobby Laverick's brief Coventry career wasn't entirely lost to history. I made one last effort, reading him his cryptic quote about dropping my father for the Oxford game, but it yielded nothing.

I had been braced for Jimmy's ruthless evaluation of my dad as past it, or the gentler explanation that he was looking to rebuild with youth and couldn't turn down a decent offer for a player who'd already turned thirty. But a ten-minute disquisition on the faults of the man he'd jettisoned my father to buy was hard to take. I thanked him and hung up.

Chapter Fourteen
Crystal Palace

IN THE OPENING DAY'S press coverage of the 1962–63 season there's a picture of my father that I've never seen before. I don't suppose it's one he would have cut out of the paper to keep.

He's lying on the ground in scene-of-the-crime posture, as though he's waiting for someone to come and chalk round him before carting him away: on his side, left arm out along the turf away from his body, right arm down towards his boots, mouth open in pain showing the gaps in his teeth.

According to the match report he'd played thirteen minutes of his debut game for Crystal Palace before being felled by 'a wince-inducing nowhere-near-the-ball tackle by brawny Burgess'. Brawny Burgess was a Canadian, and from the look of the line-up in the paper he was Halifax Town's right-half. A quick rummage in the records turns up a first name, Mike, and a career as an inside-forward that bounced around the lower divisions from Bradford Park Avenue to Aldershot. That's all I know about him, except that he signalled the beginning of the end of my father's playing career thirteen minutes into the 1962–63 season.

The move to Palace had looked like a promising one. My dad might still have been in the Third Division, but he was going to be playing for one of England's finest post-war managers: Arthur Rowe. In 1951, Rowe's Tottenham Hotspur had won the League Championship through the elegant geometry of 'push and run'. His teams kept the ball on the ground and kept it simple, passing and moving in a constantly self-reconfiguring game of join the dots. Billy Walker had built his Forest side on the Arthur Rowe model. He'd even bought one of Rowe's championship team, Eddie Baily, to play inside my father on the left. Yes, he was still in the Third Division, but he was going to be playing stylish football for a sympathetic boss.

Some of the hardest characters in the game turn out elegant, sophisticated teams, but Arthur Rowe wasn't one of them. At Tottenham he'd suffered a nervous breakdown after winning the League title, and left for the position of chief scout at West Bromwich Albion where pressure was less likely to get the better of him. Palace eventually persuaded him back into management and, despite the more physical environment of the lower end of the League, he'd taken them out of the Fourth Division playing the same kind of football that had worked in the First.

'He didn't like the term "push and run",' John Jackson, the Palace keeper, told me. 'He preferred "give it and go". One day he had us in the office and he had a bit of trelliswork, a bit of fencing. He said, "Look, football's like this" and he marked it with Biro on one bit and on another bit and he moved it and said, "Look how the pieces move in conjunction, that's how I want you to play football" – simple, very clever.'

Any expectations that moving up a division would provide a more civilised climate for Arthur Rowe's passing game had already been given a good kicking the previous season, Palace's first after promotion. Still, the Halifax Town match of 18 August 1962 seems to have been particularly brutal, even by the prevailing standards of Third Division clogging. Perhaps its ugliness was magnified because it came on the opening day of the season when – no matter how bad the previous year – a long summer of waiting fills the stands and the press box alike with hopeful amnesiacs. Whatever the reason, the reports were universal in their condemnation.

Bodies hit the deck regularly and after one tackle ex-Scottish international Stewart Imlach stayed down. And it had to be a hard tackle to make this tough bundle of energy roll in agony on the ground. Imlach limped through the rest of the match. On Monday morning he phoned Mr Rowe to say the thigh is still painful and fluid is forming on the knee.

It was a month before my father managed his second game for his new club, and his knee gave out midway through it. On 20 September, the day after my younger brother was born, he arrived home on crutches. My mother, confined to bed, had to get up to undress him and help him wash. After another six weeks of treatment a friendly was arranged against London University for him to prove his fitness in advance of Palace's 1st round FA Cup tie. Once more his knee broke down. With a new baby to look after, two other small children and yet another new house in a new city where she knew nobody, so did my mother.

'He came home on crutches again. I think I was in the middle of getting Mike ready for bed and I just screamed. I put Mike down on the carpet and put my coat on and went out.' While she walked the streets of suburban Croydon, my father stood over his youngest son like some helpless sitcom character, unable to bend down and pick up the bewildered child. The club checked him into hospital for cartilage surgery.

My mother remembers the kindness of Arthur Rowe, who knew that she was stranded and would call round in his car to pick us all up and take us to visit my father. But Arthur Rowe was on the verge of putting the baby down on the carpet and walking out himself. In the end, Palace, a family club run with paternal kindness by the chairman, Arthur Waite, recognised the symptoms and helped him to the door. At the end of November, with both team and manager struggling, they issued a statement:

The many injuries and misfortunes that have befallen the club this season have had a very adverse effect on Mr Arthur Rowe's health. The directors have therefore sent him away to recuperate until he is fit to resume office. Indeed by now he is well on his way to putting many thousands of miles between himself and club worries. We are sure the gentlemen of the press who were given evasive answers to their questions on Wednesday will forgive us and appreciate that it was only done to protect one of the greatest gentlemen in football.

'Arthur was a worrier.' Terry Long saw Palace from the Fourth Division into the First over the course of eighteen years as a player with the club. 'He liked you to play the right way, push and run all the time, and if that went bent there was nothing to fall back on. He didn't have the crunchers or what have you in the team.'

The man who took over from Rowe was his assistant, Dick Graham, a good goalkeeper for Palace until crippling back problems ended his career. 'Dick . . .' John Jackson was laughing as he flipped through the available descriptions in his mind '. . . was a different guy altogether.'

'Well, Dick was a bit of an animal,' is how his fellow keeper, Bill Glazier, put it, not without an undertone of admiration in his voice.

With Palace struggling at the lower end of the table, Arthur Rowe's elegant trelliswork was instantly dismantled in favour of a style more suited to surviving the brawny Burgesses of the Third Division. For the third time in as many clubs, my father suddenly found himself playing for a manager who hadn't signed him – and, in this case, probably had no use for him.

'Stewart was a player that Arthur Rowe liked because he was quick, he was sharp, he would give it and he would go,' Terry Long told me. 'Whereas Dick wanted lumpers and kickers and chasers and fighters, which Stewart wasn't built for. Dick had us lump it up the front to people like Cliff Holton and Peter Burridge, people who could battle and fight and knock things down.'

'I had to, I had to . . . ' Dick Graham's voice wavered a little down the phone line as he justified himself forty-odd years after the fact. 'I was convinced we had to play a more direct game. It didn't go down very well.' Not least with his own players. But Dick Graham was far more radical than his route-one approach suggests. His management philosophy was one of unsettling the opposition in any way possible, even if it meant unnerving his own team in the process, and his spell in charge at Crystal Palace was one of the strangest episodes in the club's history and my father's career.

He would play centre-forwards in the heart of the defence and wingers at full-back. When players did line up in their familiar positions he switched their shirt numbers around to fool the opposition. He refused to name his team until minutes before the kick-off, even to the people who were in it. And anyone who questioned his methods could find themselves not just dropped but cut out of club life completely.

'You never knew what was going to happen with Dick,' says Terry Long. 'You just sat there and he'd say, "So-and-so take a shirt, so-and-so take a shirt," until he got eleven and the rest of us disappeared up into the stand to watch it.'

In fact, Graham was using his first management job to test a long-held theory. 'You see, I realised that players change a lot in the lower divisions. Say you're in Division 3 and you play Swansea – the next season they could all be different players. So the easiest way to identify players was by their number. The centre-half would look and say, "Who's number 9 – that's who I've got to mark, he's the centre-forward," and I broke that down. My centre-forward would probably have number 5 on his back – and it worked. It did prove my little theory that players are used to following numbers, but I used to get slated.'

In order to implement his system, Dick Graham had to change the way teams were printed in the match programme. Until then, the traditional way of presenting the line-ups had been in team formations that showed every player's position. He had the Palace programme print the teams as a simple list. His refusal to name a team at all until he absolutely had to eventually brought about a change in Football League rules.

'He and Jimmy Hill hated each other, they really did,' said John Jackson. 'We went to Coventry and he took twenty players away with us. It wasn't a very big dressing room and he said, "No one leaves the dressing room until I say so – even those that aren't playing."

'In those days an old boy used to come to the dressing room, knock on the door and ask for the team sheet, or the team changes from the programme. Dick opens the door and he says, "I haven't got it quite ready yet, have you got theirs?" and the guy says no. He says, "Go and get theirs and then come back." So this went on all the way through, right till kick-off. We went out on the pitch and some of the guys who hadn't been picked were up in the stand sitting behind the press box. All the reporters were going, "Who's the number 7, who's the number 4?" – this was both teams – and at half-time they were still arguing about who was on the teams.'

After the game there was uproar. The Football League instructed Palace to discipline their manager. But Graham knew the rule book better than the people who'd issued it. Once they'd acknowledged that there was no regulation obliging him to declare his side in good time, the League set about creating one: team sheets were to be handed to the referee no later than half an hour before kick-off. Graham, a classic stickler, observed the new rule to the minute. Plenty of others who'd never caused the management committee a moment's bother were caught out by the change and got fined.

Training at Palace was no less strange than match day and considerably tougher. Dick Graham had the team train in army boots. He'd seen Sonny Liston on television wearing them to skip rope. Players ran with rucksacks full of sand up and down the terracing until they collapsed. Their pulses were taken to check recovery rates and to weed out anyone who'd gone down early to avoid further punishment.

George Petchey was one of the senior players and later became coach himself. 'Dick didn't have a training programme, he just did what he thought on the day. Consequently everyone was sitting round waiting to see what we were going to do, whether we needed boots, training shoes or whatever. The way he made me first-team coach was he came and said, "George, you're taking them this morning."'

John Jackson: 'He said, "I'm not going to do so much training from now on and I'm going to announce your new coach: it's George Petchey." And George is sitting there in his strip ready to train and he thought, bloody hell what's going on, I'm now the coach.

'George took us out and did the usual warm-up and Dick's standing up there – you could step out of the offices into the stands and look out over the ground – and he's watching the training and all of a sudden, like, he appears and says, "Oh, get to the back, George, and join in," and George is no longer the coach. He did crazy things, that's just how the man was.'

Dissenters went into internal exile. Terry Long was one of them: 'He made up his mind that there were players that didn't like him. We were just not part of the regime and he thought we were anti, so he wouldn't let us change in the dressing room with the rest of them, we had to go in the referee's room. Now, the referee's room wasn't very big, just a bit of a bath and a very narrow room and five or six of us had to change in there.'

In there with him was one of our neighbours, Roy Summersby, who lived in an identical club house to ours a few doors away and played golf with my father on their days off. As captain he'd gone round his teammates collecting signatures on a letter of complaint to present to the chairman. When the manager found out he was removed from the dressing room, then from the club altogether – shipped off to Portsmouth without ever playing another game for Palace.

For the first four months of the Dick Graham regime my father was a bemused spectator. His recovery from cartilage surgery was slow, painful and – although he wouldn't realise it until his playing career was over – never destined to be anything more than partial.

'It was Radley-Smith,' said my mother.

'What was?'

'Radley-Smith, he was a Harley Street specialist. It was him that made a mess of it, he left a bit in. That's why Dad was still having trouble when he was at Everton.'

I remembered the charity match knee-locks and the daily gamble of the lean forward to change channels on the television in the pre-remote control era. My dad, I discovered, had been operated on by a Brentford FC director. Eric Radley-Smith was a board member and consultant surgeon to the club. Half the repaired knee joints in the League south of Watford were his handiwork. But he'd left a bit in. After the second, remedial operation a decade later, my father had been in plaster up to his thigh and couldn't drive. He'd taken to his bike, pedalling one-legged with his left while holding the right out at an angle to avoid the rotation of the empty pedal on the other side.

In the early months of 1963, though, he was straining to get back to what he believed would be full fitness before his first season with Palace became a complete washout. He needn't have bothered. Regardless of when it was handed in, my father's name didn't appear on another Palace team sheet. Perhaps he'd ended up in the referee's room.

'Everybody fell out with Dick Graham at some stage, you had to,' said John Jackson. 'He used to hammer players, and it put players together because everybody got hammered. If he had a pop at someone after a game, we'd all be in the bath and someone would say, "Ah, take no fucking notice of him, he's an idiot." And it tended to pull players together – against the manager.'

Whatever he was then, Dick Graham now is a kindly and courteous 82-year-old, in constant pain from his back, but nonetheless keen to tell his own version of the story that everybody else is telling about him. In Dick's account he was a reluctant manager who'd been happy coaching and suffered from the stress of suddenly having to take over from Arthur Rowe. His approach had been born out of the situation Palace were in, not some brutal football philosophy. He'd been misunderstood.

The Palace players I'd spoken to – the best part of a team's worth – all seemed to have misunderstood him in pretty much the same way. The raw conflicts of their memories had been gently poached in his, and came out now as 'disagreements'. But I wasn't calling him up to cross-examine him. I just wanted to know what happened between him and my father. According to Dick Graham, nothing but football.

'Your dad was very much a push-and-run player, that was why Arthur signed him. But he had to have somebody inside him at inside-left who was used to that kind of play.

'We had Peter Burridge, an inside-left who was a quite a goal-scorer. But he was a direct player, he needed the ball in front of him, so the balance wasn't there. We needed goal-scorers so it was essential for Peter to be in, but that made it very difficult for your dad. We got Ronnie Allen from West Brom. In my wisdom I moved him and played him outside-left. He couldn't run like your dad but he used the ball like a Beckham. This helped Burridge because when the ball came Peter used to run and Ronnie Allen would drop the ball right in front of him – so it was the combination.

'But I always respected your dad's ability. I knew what he could do – I'd seen him at Forest – and your dad was what I call a true professional, y'know. He was an absolutely true pro, he got on with his training, he accepted everything and took it in good part.'

At last, a straightforward explanation, or as straightforward as one is entitled to expect. It may have been sugared slightly for my consumption; certainly it had been refracted through forty seasons of re-remembering. But the tyrant who took Arthur Rowe's vision of a side that could pass its way up the League in elegant triangles, and replaced it with the straight line of a long-ball game, had at least given me a direct answer.

My father spent all of 1963 – the rest of that first season and half of the next – in a non-playing netherworld, training for games that never came and moves that didn't materialise: *'Stewart Imlach who turned down an offer to join Chelmsford is said to have interested Fulham . . . Stewart Imlach is not to enter Southern League football after all . . . Earlier in the week Exeter made routine enquiries about Stewart Imlach . . .'*

Then, for some reason – perhaps Dick Graham was trying to confuse the opposition – he found himself back in the team early in 1964, and stayed there, on the right-wing as often as the left, as Palace pushed for promotion. Dick Graham's methods may have alienated half the team but they worked. In his first full season in charge he took Crystal Palace up into the Second Division, and my father had belatedly been a part of his strangely successful scheme. He was included in the post-season trip to Bermuda, and got the commemorative cigarette lighter for going up; it went on the windowsill, next to his Forest Cup Final ashtray.

But by Christmas 1964 he was gone. Not sold or swapped, but released and out of the League altogether. I braced myself for a hackle-raising episode of insensitivity: the back-page story that broke the news before he'd been informed, or the impersonal letter – inside the club Christmas card perhaps. Instead, I discovered what looked like an act of magnanimity. Dick Graham, knowing that he wasn't going to keep my father at the end of the season, decided to pay up his contract and let him go early. The truth may have been that the manager just wanted him out of the way – George Petchey remembers being sacked and sent home at least twice by Dick Graham – but I prefer to take the incident at face value. In two and a half seasons my father had played twenty-nine games for Palace.

Over Christmas, me and my brothers bouncing around him oblivious, he must have known the game was all but up. He'd taken his FA coaching badge while he was still at Coventry, and actually did a spell as a part-time games master at a school not far from where we lived in Croydon, teaching himself the rules of cricket and rugby from books.

But he wasn't willing just yet to let go of Saturday afternoon. He trained at Millwall and waited. He didn't have a team but at least there was some dressing-room banter to see him through the week. In early 1965 he turned out half a dozen times for Dover, then his old Coventry manager Billy Frith signed him for Southern League Chelmsford City. He wasn't short of Football League company: Tommy Wilson from Forest's Cup Final side was at centre-forward for a spell; Roy Summersby arrived to play behind him.

It was a measure of how little difference the lifting of the maximum wage had made in the lower divisions that sides like Chelmsford could compete for players. In fact, clubs much higher up the food chain were complaining about non-league teams raiding their transfer lists, signing unsettled players for no fee and depriving them of a profit. Chelmsford's application to join the league in 1965 was actually vetoed by Wolves, from whom they'd poached Bobby Mason – a player valued at £22,000 – three years earlier. The Football League brought in a five-year ban on admission for any non-league club that signed transfer-listed league players.

So the standard was probably half-decent, sort of a soccer Senior Tour or Masters Tennis with a few youngsters heading in the other direction mixed in. As a second Christmas passed without any interest from a league club, my father must have realised that this was where it was going to end. Weymouth, Bedford, Hastings, Tonbridge: his final game was going to be against one of these, perhaps without him knowing in advance that he was running out of the tunnel as a player for the last time.

Then, in the first week of 1966, just as my father turned thirty-four, Crystal Palace sacked Dick Graham. Results had been bad, but the Palace board were equally concerned by the growing pile of transfer requests from disaffected players and Graham's latest decision to dismiss George Petchey as first-team coach. Arthur Rowe, who'd stayed on the payroll doing a little scouting, was re-installed as the team figurehead, with Petchey recalled as his assistant to share the stress and take the coaching.

A fortnight after taking over, Arthur Rowe asked the Palace board for permission to sign my father for a second time. 'I should very much like to have him back. He is a good honest character and tries hard all the time. He will be a good influence to our youngsters and apprentices with whom he will be mixing.'

After some discussion the directors agreed to pay Chelmsford £1,000 for the man whose contract they'd paid up thirteen months earlier. The idea was that he would help to bring on Palace's promising crop of young players, combining appearances in the reserves with the start of a coaching career. Instead, he went straight into the first team and stayed there until the end of the season, turning in a string of dazzling performances so implausible it was almost as though his teammates were too dumbstruck to capitalise on them: 'IMLACH INSPIRATION WASTED', 'IMLACH SO NEAR TO TAKING BOTH POINTS FOR PALACE', 'OH THOSE MISSED CHANCES, SIGHS SPEEDY IMLACH.'

After three and a half seasons of being tagged on to the end of match reports as an injury update or a transfer rumour, my father spent February to May 1966 in 24-point type. It was like a long-delayed retake. This was the season he was supposed to have had when he arrived in 1962; could have had if it hadn't been for brawny Burgess.

Then it might still have led to something more than just the end of his career. Now he must have known it wouldn't be long before he walked down the tunnel and peeled off permanently towards the boot room instead of the dressing room. But instead of finding – like so many players before and after him – that his top-flight career was over before he'd had time to appreciate it, I like to think that events conspired to make it impossible for my father not to appreciate his.

No one limps down into non-league football on a badly repaired knee then gets summoned back for a Second Division curtain call at the age of thirty-four. The six-year game of pass-the-parcel that Billy Walker started at the end of the 1959–60 season had seen my father fall into some unsympathetic hands. But Arthur Rowe, whose plans for him the first time round had been postponed by injury and ill health, contrived at least to let him come back and say goodbye to the professional game properly.

My view of the Palace manager may be clouded by sentimentality, but from four decades away it looks like a piece of benign plotting on his part. He persuaded the board to take my father back as a coach, then picked him for the first team the week he arrived. He coaxed from him a string of wonderful performances that my dad probably didn't believe he was still capable of. He even made my father captain for a friendly against Nottingham Forest in which he led the team to a 4–1 win. It couldn't have been more like a farewell tour if the club shop had been selling team bomber jackets with his crew-cut caricature on the back.

Second Division Crystal Palace, not Southern League Chelmsford City, would be the final club on my dad's playing CV. Sadly, Arthur Rowe wouldn't be his last manager. Early in April 1966, a few weeks after the Forest friendly, the stress of football management became too much for him again and he asked to be relieved of his duties.

*   *   *

The 1965–66 season didn't so much end as segue straight into the World Cup. Football was well established as the nation's favourite game, but this was the first time it had shown serious signs of colonising the cricket season. Its players were heroes, but television had yet to turn them into full-blown celebrities. 1966 was the year it set about the task in earnest.

On 24 May, the BBC aired the pilot of a show called *Quiz Ball*. Teams of four representing a club – three players and a star guest – were tested on their general knowledge by David Vine, with the winners progressing through knockout rounds to a grand final at the end of the series. It ran for five years, before giving up the popularity battle with *A Question of Sport* and slipping into an obscurity beyond the reach of even TV list programmes.

It did, though, make one enduring contribution to the vocabulary of the game: Route One. When the Palace players complained to me about Dick Graham's tactics, they were using a term that hadn't existed when he first screamed at them from the dugout to stop fannying about and get the ball upfield. Route One was the direct path to goal on David Vine's large electronic football pitch, a single all-or-nothing gamble on getting the right answer. Route Four was the Arthur Rowe approach, a series of simpler questions strung together towards the same end. Palace actually reached the final of *Quiz Ball* in the late '60s, although sadly there's no record of whose tactics they used.

There's no surviving footage either of my father's appearance on the very first show, but he did keep his copy of the contract, signed by the Head of Artists Bookings, Bush Bailey. The fee was twenty-five guineas, almost certainly the only time in his life that he was paid in the denomination of the upper classes. Guineas were for gentlemen not players. The sum – still a week's wages or the best part of it for many of the League's footballers – must have opened his eyes too. There was more on offer here for turning up and simply *being* a footballer for an hour or so than he'd been able to earn sweating at the business of playing football for most of the weeks of his career.

There was no benefit match when my father stopped playing – he'd never stayed anywhere long enough to merit one. In any case there was no official announcement or date to hang it on, just a slow fade off the team sheet and on to the coaching staff. But his last recorded appearance in a Crystal Palace shirt was a testimonial in October 1966, for his teammate Terry Long.

The timing – in the long afterglow of the World Cup – and the quality of the opposition ensured a packed house and a decent profit once the groundstaff had been paid. George Cohen was there from the World Cup-winning team along with fellow England squad members Jimmy Greaves, George Eastham and Ron Springett. Johnny Haynes turned out; so did the former Palace favourite Johnny Byrne, and a sprinkling of Chelsea stars like Eddie McCreadie, Marvin Hinton and Bobby Tambling.

Listed in the paper but not the match programme was Sir Stanley Matthews. He had demanded a fee that would have put a serious dent in the night's takings. The maximum wage had been unfair on every professional footballer, but on him perhaps more than most. There were old players I'd spoken to who still sounded less aggrieved at having suffered under the maximum than they did guilty for having taken home the same money as Stan Matthews every week. At least he hadn't retired the year before it was lifted, like Tom Finney. But then Finney had stopped playing when he was thirty-eight. Matthews only earned a belated fraction of what he was worth by carrying on until he was fifty.

In 1965 he'd become the first footballer ever to be knighted, the same year that George Best opened his first boutique. Then he'd watched England's World Cup winners step straight off the field at

Wembley into a world of vast and widening commercial opportunity. Stan had managed his fair share of endorsements during his long playing career, but nothing like this. Sitting at home with his knighthood and seeing what younger, lesser players were earning made him very conscious of his own market worth, and determined not to undercut it. So, Sir Stan wasn't there for Terry Long's testimonial – he left it to the new generation flush enough to turn out for expenses.

At most levels of the game the benefit match has become an anachronism at best, at worst a borderline obscenity. For Terry Long it meant a degree of security after ten seasons' service. 'It enabled me to buy the house I'm talking to you from now,' he told me over the phone. 'In those days you didn't want to have a mortgage because you didn't know when your £20 a week was going to finish, so rather than have a mortgage and worry about getting sacked from football and thinking, what are we going to do?, we thought we'll buy the house without the mortgage and at least we've got somewhere to live.'

Terry cleared just over £4,000, although it could have been more. It was the first testimonial game Palace had ever staged. They guessed at the likely crowd and printed 12,000 programmes, but more than 17,000 people turned up. The game was the usual goal feast, with the fans treated to the novelty of endless personnel changes. According to the match report, 'Stewart Imlach came on for 45 minutes and was as popular as ever with the crowd.' The final score was 7–5 to the Internationals. My dad got Palace's fifth in the eighty-sixth minute. 'It must have been him that got in my way then because they were trying to let me score. Y'know what it's like on testimonial nights – they're all trying to tee it up and you sort of trip over it or mishead it or something. I never did score.'

Terry Long spent another seven seasons at Selhurst Park after his testimonial, but it was my father's farewell game. He wouldn't have known that then, but I know and I have no compunction about hijacking it for him: co-opting Greaves and Haynes and Eastham to his cause, all of them turning out to make sure that my dad's last match was against opposition of the highest possible quality; football's first £100-a-week player applauding him back to the halfway line after he'd knocked in the final goal of his final game; the man who took on the retain-and-transfer system shaking hands with him at the whistle and wishing him all the best.

There's no mention in the match report of who was in the crowd, but I put Arthur Rowe in the directors' box, happy and relaxed. Not worrying about the result for once, just enjoying the game.

Chapter Fifteen
Coaching

THE DEAD ALL HAVE their regular spots at Goodison Park. I can't remember seeing any when we used to walk around the ground as kids, but the place is full of them now.

Percy Harwood (1904–2001, Goodison Regular 1913–2000) is behind the goal at the Park End, just along from John Wagstaff (Age 67, Simply The Best). The narrow wooden skirting that surrounds the field has a cordon of commemorative plaques, facing back towards the crowd like stewards on match day. Ashes are usually scattered in the centre circle or the goalmouths; players taking throw-ins stand over the urns buried around the perimeter. All but one are fans. Of the men who graced the pitch in life, only Everton's first great goalkeeper, Ted Sagar, has come back to be interred beneath it. Still, it's popular enough as a final resting place that the ground-staff have had to call a halt. Season tickets for eternity are sold out.

My father's ashes went on Formby Golf Course, the one club that never sacked or sold him. His career, though, like so many careers of his generation, had finished back at ground level. Groundsman level. The old man marking out the pitch or putting up the nets – barely noticed by the kids eager to get on with their game and ignorant of his brilliant past – has become a stock character. A period character too. The reason so many men of that era stayed in the game is because they had nowhere else to go. Playing football for a living is famously poor preparation for doing anything else, and the stories are legion of players who found that once the exoskeleton of the game had been removed, their lives were as shapeless and vulnerable as some sea-jelly without its shell.

For every man like my father with a marketable trade and a willingness to use it, there were others who never planned ahead, couldn't face any of the alternatives to playing, and went down fast once their celebrity – and their money if they'd managed to save any – ran out. I vaguely remember the hand-wringing there'd been over Tommy Lawton at Notts County when I was seven or eight. My dad wasn't keen on calling in the police to deal with the club's most illustrious ex-player. But when things started disappearing from the pockets of County's teenage trialists as well as from the coaches' room, there'd been no choice.

As late as 1967 my father had still had been registered as a player with Crystal Palace. But he was effectively coaching full-time when the offer came in March that year to return to Nottingham as assistant manager with Notts County.

It wasn't just a footballing move; here was a chance for my parents to return to the community where they'd felt most at home and plan for a life beyond the game. My father invested his entire savings from football in a friend's chain of newsagents, with a view to the pair of them going into partnership. He even did a spell behind the counter while he was still at Meadow Lane to prepare for the transition. But the partnership didn't materialise and the cash was never returned.

I can't imagine him running a shop anyway, not for long. For my father, football wasn't an escape from growing up like it is for some players, but it was, I think, an escape from growing bitter or frustrated. When he left the game to work outside full-time, his impatience and intolerance of fools could be things of corrosive, ulcer-forming intensity. I'm sure it wasn't that his patience had never been tried by fools inside football – just that the game itself had always been there to save him: an outlet for frustration, a glorious distraction and a simple, unpolluted pleasure which never failed him, whether it was ninety minutes on a Saturday or half an hour's five-a-side to finish training. Perhaps his erstwhile friend did him a kind of cruel favour – condemning him to years longer in the game where he'd be happier and poorer.

After two years back in Nottingham he took the offer to step down to youth coach and up to the First Division with Everton. In 1969 the final wishes of lifelong fans had yet to overwhelm the groundstaff and, despite the Jags in the players' parking spaces, Everton's famously authoritarian manager Harry Catterick ran the kind of regime that hadn't changed since my father's playing days, or possibly Catterick's own.

Everyone – from the England internationals to the apprentices coming by bus – had to sign in each morning in a massive blue ledger at the entrance to Bellefield, Everton's training ground. When the deadline passed, the pencil was replaced by a red pen. It wasn't quite the time-clock at Cammell Laird, but there were fines for anyone whose name the manager could read in Biro. He weighed them every Friday. There was a lock on the television in the lounge. If Alan Ball and Howard Kendall wanted to play table tennis, they had to go to Jean, the manager's secretary, to ask for the ball just like we did. And take it back afterwards.

Catterick's brilliance lay in buying and blending. Once he had the people in place he let them get on with it – obliged them to get on with it. He rarely materialised at training-ground level, but from his corner office on the first floor he could see all the parts of Bellefield that mattered; the slightest change in the angle of the blinds in his window was enough to quicken the pace down below. This was the evolutionary shuffle by which football clubs moved forward, half behind the times, half ahead; the generation that could no longer play working to stamp its values on the next, and competing vicariously through fresh legs. Methods were handed down, amended, rejected, diluted, and eventually the pimply apprentices became the grizzled occupants of the boot room or the upstairs office. Depending on their status, the supplanted generation moved into venerated retirement, slipped back into the mass of fans, or returned to the ground to lay turf and scatter ashes.

Ronnie Goodlass and my father went through the ranks together, player and coach, from the youth team to the first team, both of them wingers. Long after my father had left the club his relentless disciplinarian enthusiasm was still echoing off the gym walls at Bellefield, channelled through Goodlass's own experience, and influencing a generation of apprentices who wouldn't have known the man if they'd walked past him. Which, of course, they did. My father's final job before retirement was looking after Littlewoods' Recreation Grounds in Bootle; a bleak corner plot of football pitches and tennis courts that the traffic largely ignores on its way to Aintree Racecourse, or the match.

Everton began to use it as an occasional overspill from Bellefield for the youth teams. The teenagers didn't know him, but their coaches did and would stop to talk. He and Colin Harvey might compare notes on the state of their hips – my father was already one replacement joint down the road that Colin was limping along. The PFA had helped him pay for it.

Relentlessly practical, he had refused a general anaesthetic, preferring to remain conscious while they hacked the crumbling joint away and replaced it with titanium and polythene. He'd heard that this was the best way to shorten your recovery time, because a surgeon was always gentler on patients who could keep their eye on proceedings. As he told the joke against himself afterwards, he'd dozed off anyway only to be disturbed some time later by a terrible racket, some workmen in the distance: 'Christ, I thought, what's that bloody hammering?' It was the surgeon taking a chisel to his pelvis.

It didn't stop him chasing the local kids, who would make holes in the fence at Littlewoods and commit whatever acts of petty vandalism they could get away with before they were spotted.

Inevitably, when he finally caught one and administered the summary justice he'd felt round the ear himself from the local bobby in Lossiemouth, he was the one in the wrong. He couldn't see it, but the boy's family called the police and in the end he had to go and apologise to avoid going to court.

This old-fashioned, small-town outlook was the face he presented to the world regardless of who was watching. It had been sketched for readers of the Liverpool *Daily Post* in 1973, when he was still the first-team coach at Everton. It was a period of relatively easy journalistic access; after football's original Victorian rules of privacy had been lifted and before the later corporate regimes had brought them slamming back down again. The previous year Hunter Davies had published his classic inside story of a season with Spurs, *The Glory Game*. To start the new season, the *Daily Post* sent in their man Erlend Clouston to do something similar over a few weeks with Everton for a string of features:

> Imlach, a dark-haired wiry little Scot, is a humorous, sympathetic man, mysteriously obliged by fate to show the world the worried, affronted expression of a man who has been caught with nothing less than 50p when the collecting plate came round.

> Stewart . . . still preserves the countryman's quaint vision of the universe. I came from the Shetland Islands did I? Well I must have known Peter Walterson, a policeman in Lerwick.

'Aye, well he did,' was my father's only comment on the piece. Erlend Clouston would never have got near pre-season training when Harry Catterick was there, but Catterick had just been replaced by the slick and media-conscious Billy Bingham, who immediately set about his predecessor's fixtures and fittings. The lock came off the television, ping-pong balls abounded and the signing-in book was decommissioned. My dad brought it home: probably one of the largest collections of Everton autographs in existence, all adding up to the giant signature of the one name not in the book.

It's a record of Harry Catterick's last twelve months in the job, starting in April 1972 with the words NURSING HOME printed across a week's worth of the spaces reserved for the signatures of Joe Royle and Alan Whittle – he was two strikers down. Whittle's sequence resumes, only to end abruptly on Saturday 9 December. On Monday the 11th the box next to his squad number has a diagonal line through it, under which my father has written *C. Palace*. The space for David Johnson's signature goes blank for a month and then the surname changes; Johnson had been sold to Ipswich, Joe Harper had arrived from Aberdeen to take his place in the team and the book.

The changing entries for squad number 26 chart the peaks and troughs of Joe Royle's season, and his battle with chronic back pain: ENGLAND one week, HOSPITAL the next. When he's late he signs himself Joseph, letting the boss know how 4th Form he thinks the system is, but not so blatantly as to get his fine doubled. He's a future occupant of the upstairs office. Along with the red-pen entries of the honestly late, there are some suspicious-looking efforts in pencil, where an apprentice has been bribed or threatened into forging a senior player's name.

The strength of Catterick's personality is underlined by how long the book survives him. He was 'moved to administrative duties' on 12 April 1973, but the pages are full well into the off-season when attendance would have been voluntary anyway except for the injured. Howard Kendall and Tommy Wright are among those still signing in towards the end of June. Fittingly, the final, lone entry on 5 July belongs to Mick Lyons, a fanatical throwback who had to be ordered home to prevent him from training round the clock.

My father would have approved of Catterick's emphasis on punctuality. Being kept waiting was the one thing guaranteed to set him twitching. He shared the drive into training with two of the other coaches who lived in Formby. He was never a minute late collecting them, and would be standing in the bay window jingling his change well in advance of his own scheduled pick-up time. In his book, poor timekeeping was the tip of an iceberg's worth of disrespect, and his response was usually in proportion to the invisible four-fifths. Not long before his illness was diagnosed, my mother had turned round as she prepared tea to see him standing with his hands on the back of his chair at the dining table, trembling with suppressed irritation as the second hand on his watch edged past his designated meal-time.

'Stewart, you're retired, what does it matter?'

'Time's all I've got.'

It had stuck in her mind as an unusually cryptic, not to say philo-sophical, thing for my father to come out with. As though he'd sensed the onset of his cancer. Perhaps he was just giving voice, and probably for the first time in his life, to the shapeless fear of being an ex-something. Football had structured his life into seasons and weeks and forty-five-minute parcels of purpose. Now, tee-times and mealtimes were his only points of reference. I imagine anyone in his foursome who kept him waiting on the first at Formby got the same treatment.

Towards the end of his life he seemed to be in the service of his watch. It was a chunky stainless-steel Seiko that had no battery, but stored and used the kinetic energy of the wearer, the perfect model for my father. Even sitting watching television he was never still, his legs shooting out every so often like a jumpy driving instructor going for the dual controls. But eventually it became too heavy for him to wear. And in any case he'd fallen below the threshold of movement required to keep the hands turning. So once or twice a day he'd gather what energy he had and transfer it to the watch – picking it up by the strap and swinging his arm slowly back and forth by the side of his chair. When he was satisfied that he had enough time in the bank, enough for another twelve or fourteen hours, he'd place it on the coffee table again and sit back to recover from the effort.

Timekeeping was one of the few responsibilities Billy Bingham left him with. Harry Catterick's tracksuit had come out exactly as often as the team photographer did; Bingham wore his every day. He did the coaching, my father did the training and kept the players organised. He was the one who went round to check they were all in their rooms during away trips, on the pretext of handing out sleeping pills. Plenty of managers would have brought an entire staff with them, so perhaps he felt lucky not to have been cleared out altogether, along with the signing-in book. And since it fell into the category of things he could do nothing about, he seems simply to have got on with what was left of his job. His training books are careful and thorough. Should Martin Dobson or Bob Latchford ever want to check their mid-1970s bodyweights, bench-press performances or distances for the twelve-minute run, I'd be able to help them.

His entry for Saturday 3 January 1976 records the Everton line-up for the 3rd Round FA Cup tie away at Derby, notes John Connolly's appearance as a substitute for the last fifteen minutes and Gary Jones's goal in a 2–1 defeat. There's a two-line summary: *Gave away silly goal early on and took time to settle. Great second half and did everything but score.* The next page is headed: *12th July, Pre-Season Training Blackpool, '76/77.*

My father wouldn't have appreciated it and the manager wouldn't have admitted to it, but there's no avoiding the irony of his sacking by Bingham: first being stripped of responsibility for the way the team played, then being made to carry the can for it. Two weeks later Bingham survived the dreaded vote of confidence from the

Everton chairman, and hung on into the following season before being sacked himself.

January 3 and July 12 1976 are consecutive days in my dad's book, as though the intervening six months had been cancelled through lack of football. He'd been sacked the day before his forty-fourth birthday, the age I am now, writing about him. I'm trying – unsuccessfully – to put myself in a similar position, and imagine how I'd react and what I'd do. He signed on at Liverpool docks as a joiner and started work at the Pier Head – not closeted away in a workshop, but in full view of the passengers filing on and off the Mersey ferries. Inevitably he was spotted.

THE MAN WITH THE HAMMER, was the headline in the *Daily Post*, and there he was next to it, knocking a nail into a piece of wood. It was the companion shot to the one of him sawing at his workbench published in the Bury *Times* nearly a quarter of a century earlier. The first depicted a young man on the verge of leaving his apprenticed trade for a life in football, the second marked the return journey. I seem to remember the photograph being taken at the house. It's certainly framed to keep the background neutral, and doesn't really stand up to the 'thousands-of-commuters-cast-hardly-a-glance/how-the-mighty-are-fallen' line of the piece.

My dad would have been happy to oblige the photographer, but I'm not sure he'd really have been able to fathom the reason for the *Post*'s interest in the first place. Times had changed, but he hadn't. The papers had never bothered in Nottingham when he was putting up Wall's Ice Cream signs or working at the Co-op depot in the off-season – why were they making all this fuss now?

According to the story, he'd turned down several offers to sell his side of it. In fact, none of his quotes in the papers around the time of the sacking stray much beyond 'That's football'. Which it was. The game hadn't taken over the feature sections and the showbiz pages then – not that either of them would have been interested in this particular episode. But scandal stories were pretty easily contained because clubs, for the most part, had only the football writers to worry about. And the football writers, although they now had proper bylines instead of careers disguised as Ranger or Free Forester, still operated under essentially the same agreement: a free run in return for a blind eye.

There are much more salacious examples from that period than the exploits of Bernie Wright – players summarily shipped off to other clubs to avoid the scandalous whiff of rumours about sex with underage girls – but Bernie had a direct impact on my dad. He was one of Harry Catterick's rare mistakes, signed after scoring at Goodison for Third Division Walsall in a cup tie in 1972. A strong, crude centre-forward – Bernie the Bolt – he was nineteen years old and had played only fifteen games as a professional. He managed ten more in eleven months at Everton before being released for 'serious misconduct'. That, from the ex-players I've talked to, consisted of going on a bender with the contents of the annual Christmas hamper that the chairman, John Moores, gave to every player, and trying to confront a rattled Catterick, who escaped out of the back door. The signing-in book shows his name dissolving from legibility into a nonsensical squiggle over the course of a couple of months, before disappearing for good on 21 December.

Before then, though, he'd already laid my father out in training. The reserves and the first team did their warm-up jogs in opposite directions around Bellefield. Catterick decided who was in which group, and told his coaches before the morning began. My father, having announced who was training where, set off one way with the first-teamers. Gordon West, who'd lost his place in goal but was still the club's top mischief-maker, was in the reserve group with Bernie Wright, relentlessly winding him up about how disgraceful it was that a player like him should be down with the dead men, what an insult it was to his talent and ability. Bernie couldn't help but agree, and became more agitated with every step. As the two groups completed a circuit and passed each other, Wright went for my father, felling him with a meaty fist to the face. Gordon West was the first player in to pull him off. But the papers didn't get my father's side of that story, or any side of it. Which isn't to say that their staff writers didn't.

Having been sacked by one of the Luton team he had helped defeat at Wembley in 1959, it was odd that my father should be thrown a lifeline by another. But Allan Brown, his union rep at Luton and fellow Scottish international, was a friend, and their first season together as manager and assistant at Blackpool was a successful one. Agonisingly so, in fact, although you wouldn't know from the deadpan entry in his book for Saturday 14 May, the final day of the 1976–77 season: *Missed promotion by a point, due mainly to our failure to win enough home games. Away record was very good. We were better equipped to defend and punish teams on the break. Not enough flair to beat defensive teams at home. Badly needed a winger.*

Blackpool were in the Second Division when my dad joined forces with Allan Brown. The fans must have had high hopes that they could go a point better by the end of the following season, but the partnership didn't survive that long.

All his playing life, club directors had decided where he should live and work, sending him pinballing from the north-west through the Midlands down to the Home Counties and back up again. Formby to Blackpool was an easy commute – you could see the Tower from Formby beach on a half-decent day – but the Blackpool board wanted him to move. Perhaps it had been an implicit part of the deal when he first signed. My parents went through the motions of looking at houses without much enthusiasm. None of us wanted to go. My father tried to placate the club by living with Allan Brown and his family during the week, returning on Saturday nights after the match for half a weekend at home. But they insisted, and he refused. He got a job installing double-glazing.

The following summer he asked me to help him out for a couple of days on a job at a house in Litherland, along the route we used to take to Goodison Park. I had an A-level exam on one of the days and should have been revising on the other, but he didn't know that. His role in my education was that of enforcer, wheeled in to mete out the punishment when my mother found undelivered school reports at the back of the wardrobe. In any case, I was pretty sure I was going to fail, so this at least was a way to avoid two hours in the school gym failing in person.

He didn't really need me, except for a couple of very large panes in upstairs windows. We had to edge up gently with them on parallel ladders and ease the heavy rectangles into place, then he'd scuttle down his ladder leaving me swaying slightly at the top of mine, both hands pressing flat on the pane, while he got the rubber beading to secure it. The rest of the time, I fetched or handed him things, and went for the KitKats for our break. I couldn't picture myself ever having this kind of confidence or competence. When we'd pulled the old windows out, frames and all, to leave nothing but a gaping hole of jagged brickwork in the living-room bay, I had been terrified. How the hell were we going to fill this? But he'd measured the job weeks earlier, and where the factory had made a mistake or forgotten to send some small part of the kit, he'd improvise, just get on with it, like he got on with things in general.

Whether it was due to his age, a growing concern for what my mother wanted, unwillingness to disrupt our education, or a combination of the lot, home life began to get the upper hand over football. Starting with his departure from Everton, he turned down a number of jobs that would have meant another move: national coach of British Guyana (vetoed by my mother before any of us could get excited); assistant to Peter Taylor at Brighton (entertained, but eventually declined).

The job we all would have moved for was a position on the coaching staff at Nottingham Forest. Brian Clough called, my father drove down, we held our breath, and he drove back. Clough had kept him waiting, like he kept everybody waiting, like he would have kept a delegation of Pelé, Puskas and Stan Matthews waiting. My father had sat and twitched and jingled his change, and eventually asked Clough's secretary where he was. She made the mistake of telling the truth, which was that he was playing squash, and my father got in his car and came home. Clough called the next day to tell him the job was his anyway. My father told him to stuff it and hung up. Just as well for both of them, really. They'd managed to telescope into twenty-four hours a relationship that would have ended exactly the same way two weeks or two months later.

That was the end of his chance to return to the ground where he'd played his best football and finish his career helping the next Forest generation play theirs. Instead, his final coaching job completed a different circle, one that led back to his first club. Some of the Blackpool players had recommended him to Dave Hatton, an ex-Blackpool player himself, who needed a veteran coach to help him in his first job as player-manager at Bury.

When my father arrived back at Gigg Lane in the summer of 1978, twenty-four years after he'd left, Les Hart was still there. He had already been there fourteen years when my father first signed in 1952. Back then Hart was the Bury centre-half. Since, he'd been trainer, physio, then manager for a season, before retreating back into the brickwork. Les Hart saw my father leave the second time; the players presented him with a retirement watch and silver salver in March 1980, a few months after manager and coach had both been dismissed.

Bury, at least, sacked my dad over poor results, although for some reason it went down in the boardroom minutes as a cost-cutting measure. To begin with, he and Dave Hatton had enjoyed solid support from the Bury chairman, Bill Allen. But Allen collapsed and died of a heart attack shovelling snow at the ground during the winter of their first season in charge. His successor, Ron Clarke, was more abrasive. In the directors' lounge after one poor performance he asked my father whether the team ever actually practised taking corners during training. The reply was a short lecture on the respective job descriptions of club chairman and team coach, with emphasis on how little overlap there was between them.

My father had been a clever player, and as a coach he was a good tactician. If things were going badly out on the field he could see the underlying reasons and knew what adjustments to make. But in life he lacked guile. He didn't have the talent or the patience for office politics, he couldn't compromise. Off the field his only tactic was being right, and when that failed he had nothing to fall back on. At Bury there was no arguing with the league table: nineteenth in his only full season there; six points from eleven games to start the next.

My father was forty-seven when he left football for good, and except for trips to watch Mike play, I don't think he went to another professional match. He followed the game in general and on television, but individual matches were things he'd only ever attended in order to contribute. Before finishing up as the groundsman at Littlewoods, he took an uninspiring job with a video-hire company and dabbled in the post-game career choice he'd declared all those years previously in the Forest Cup Final souvenir magazine: '*a return to the joinery business*'. Some of his work is still visible around Formby – garden gates, carports, front doors – the details logged in the back of one of his half-filled training books.

In that pre-cup final questionnaire only two of the Forest team had said they planned to stay in the game once they'd finished playing: Jack Burkitt, although he was hedging his bets by '*learning the lace trade*'; and Billy Gray, who wanted to become '*an FA coach or a school sports master*'. In fact, the majority of them stayed in the game as long as they could, at whatever level they could. Only three of the side – Bill Whare, Jeff Whitefoot and Chic Thomson – walked away from football when they finished playing, and two of those walked into pubs, which perhaps doesn't fully count as leaving. Chic became a social worker.

Jack Burkitt coached at Forest then took the manager's job at Notts County. He was trainer at Derby County when Brian Clough took them into the First Division, then left the game to run a post office. Billy Gray managed Millwall, Brentford and Notts County, where he employed my father, and eventually returned to Meadow Lane to end his career as head groundsman.

Bob McKinlay (*training to be a motor mechanic*) was with my father and Jack Burkitt on the same FA Preliminary Coaching Course at Lilleshall in 1961, along with the likes of Noel Cantwell and Maurice Setters from Manchester United and West Brom's Bobby Robson. Bob's coaching career at the City Ground lasted only a few months, just long enough to be sacked when Dave Mackay took over as manager. He spent the rest of his career in the prison service.

Tommy Wilson (*to become a shopkeeper*) managed Brentwood, then became a children's group leader. Joe McDonald (*sewing machine mechanic*) was at Yeovil Town before leaving the game and the country for Australia. Johnny Quigley (*running his own business*) left the country for a spell but stayed in the game, coaching in Kuwait and Saudi Arabia. Roy Dwight (*the confectionery business*) had five years in charge of Tooting & Mitcham. He finally led them to the FA Cup 3rd Round giant-kill that Forest had denied them: in 1976 they beat Swindon to register their best ever cup result. He ended up as the manager of Crayford Dog Track in Kent, fielding occasional press enquiries about his more famous piano-playing cousin, Reg Dwight.

The most frequent reminder of their playing days for the survivors of that team now is the steady trickle of requests they get from memorabilia collectors or, more likely, memorabilia traders. The men I went to see had all been visited by the same one, or had received sheaves of photos through the post from him to be signed and sent back. 'God, this guy came round – I must have been here three hours signing autographs. It was the same the other night in the pub, some fella – "Are you Johnny Quigley, d'you mind if I send some photos and can you autograph them?" I said yeah.'

If Chic Thomson had the best memory of anyone my father played with, Johnny Quigley had the fiercest. He had made his debut in the crucible of Forest's 1957 game against Manchester United, supplying the cross for my father to score, and the intensity of that day never seemed to have left him. I'd been warned that he was in poor health, had recently suffered a stroke; there was speculation about how well he was managing to make a living, or whether he was making one at all. But we talked about football, and he spoke as though the adrenalin was still pumping through him from a game that had finished half an hour ago. His accent was as broad as my father's, a proud Glaswegian, and the opinions came in staccato bursts.

'Some runner your old man, I'll tell you – he could fly, quickest thing I've seen . . .

'The guy Baily – he was a genius, to me. And he could put the ball where your dad wanted it . . .

'Joe McDonald, smoked all the time. Smoked under the shower, man, and never got the cigarette wet. Unbelievable. Good player, mind . . .

'People think Cloughie made Forest a footballing team – Forest were a football-playing team long before Cloughie was invented . . .

'It's not the same passion. The crowd's got the passion, but years ago the players used to have the passion as well. We was a part of the fans . . .'

He was equally forceful on the subject of players' earnings, the current state of the Scotland team and the regular attentions of the autograph merchants – although he always obliged them. 'It's not as if you sign one or two, there's twenty, and the guy says, "Oh, this is the last three." It's not the last one, mind, it's the last three. Some of the photographs he had, I've never seen them before.'

Johnny Quigley had precisely two photographs from his days as a player. Both of them hung in the hall of his small, tidy flat, the only signs that the place had a long-term tenant. 'There was an old lady, she came and said, "You were my favourite player, here's a photograph for you," and she gave me a photograph – Cynthia, she was called. I used to have an album, but when I parted with my missus she gave it to my lad Damon. I've never seen anything since. Photos of when I played with the juniors in Scotland before I came down here, but I don't know what he's done with it.'

A lot of the Forest players hadn't bothered to keep the Cup Final newspapers because the club had promised each of them a scrapbook. But the scrapbooks never arrived, and now they get knocks on the door and large manila envelopes through the post from people who own pictures of them that they don't own themselves. And they sign them and send them back because that's the courteous thing to do, and because it's what they've always done, and because, I suppose, they're being remembered, even if it is by someone who's trying to make money off them. I wondered whether the men with the manila envelopes ever asked to see his medal.

'I don't know where mine is. When I left my missus, I left her with everything. I think my lad's got the tracksuit and the jersey and that.'

The other surviving members of the Forest team I talked to didn't know where theirs were either: they'd been sold. I was shocked. I knew Bob McKinlay had sold his medal before he died, reportedly back to the club, although there was no medal on display at the City Ground and no record of them having one. Then there was the anonymous player in the *Evening Post* story that someone had cut out and sent to my father not long before he died. But I had thought they were the exceptions. In fact, there were no medals to see on my trip to Nottingham.

Chic Thomson was happy he'd offloaded his. He and a few of his old Chelsea teammates had been approached about selling their 1954–55 League Championship medals at auction, and he'd decided to get rid of everything in one go. 'I had two boys, three medals with Clyde, army medal, league medal, cup medal. Who gets what? I didn't want to cause any trouble. I talked it over with Pat and chatted with the boys and said whatever we get we'll split it down the middle and you can share it out.'

He had sat at Bonhams and watched it all go. His cup final jersey, nicely framed, fetched £1,000. Someone paid £600 for his tracksuit top. The cup winner's medal went for £3,500, no match for a league title at a big, metropolitan showbiz club: his Chelsea medal topped out at £13,000. By the time it was all added up, the material evidence of Chic's career came in at a couple of hundred pounds under £20,000.

'Pat had to go out because it was getting crazy. But I said to the lads, "I would have liked to have had a lump sum like that when I was forty-five." It cleared the air. I was always a bit bothered about what we'd do with them.'

I admired Chic's elegant clean sweep of his football history, but it saddened me too. He hadn't done it out of necessity, or for himself;

it had been his choice, to provide for his sons. But there isn't the son of a player with even half Chic's achievements who would need that provision today. And the archaeology of his career, a single fabulous trove that held his whole story intact, was now scattered among strangers. My reaction was partly selfish, too, because his story was part of my father's, just as my father's was part of his.

After its fifteen years or so in the daylight hanging on the living-room wall, my father's medal had been back in its leather box long enough to form a greenish ellipse on the silk lining over the address of Fattorini & Sons, the Bradford gold and silversmiths who also made the FA Cup. I can't think of circumstances that would have forced him to sell it. That is to say I can, but they fall into the emergency-lifesaving-operation-abroad-for-my-mother category. He'd have scuffled through an impecunious old age, if it had ever come to that, without the thought once entering his head.

Johnny Quigley didn't even have his history to sell if he'd wanted to. He followed me to the door, to drive home one last point.

'It's good to speak to a friend of mine's son,' he said, and gripped me by the hand.

'It's good to speak to you, John.'

Chapter Sixteen
Capped

INCLUDED IN THE SQUAD, picked for the first team, capped by your country. The escalating terminology of recognition in football culminates literally at the top. Footballers don't play for their national sides, they're capped. Caps are part of the language, the elite currency of the game. They're the final, bluff-calling card in any dressing-room dispute: 'Oh yeah? – how many caps have you got, then?'

And as every schoolboy learns in his introduction to the fabulous world of football cliché, the only way to collect them is one game at a time. That's the rule: a cap for every international appearance until the day the photographers arrive and ask you to spread them out on the living-room carpet, or in the back garden.

But my father didn't have one. It was like a trick question, a pub-quiz tiebreaker: 'How is it possible to play for your country without getting capped?' My father knew the answer: he was the answer. The only time I saw him court recognition of any kind was in his pursuit of a cap. He'd represented his country – at a World Cup no less – yet never received one. Now they were dishing them out to players with estuary English accents and suspiciously grafted-looking branches on their family trees. Players could pick up a cap for coming on ten minutes from the end of a pointless friendly. How come they all had caps and he didn't? The explanation was depressingly straightforward. At the time he played, the Scottish FA – stereotypically thrifty in a way my father might have approved of in principle – awarded caps only for games against the other home countries.

In fact, to be strictly accurate, they economised even on this basic token of recognition, handing out just one cap per player per year for all home internationals. My father's World Cup teammate John Hewie appeared nineteen times for his country, including six home internationals in 1956, '57 and '59. He got three caps. 'Yes, they'd give you one cap at the end of the season, and on it in gold braid you would have S v E, S v I, S v W for whichever countries you'd played against. The English and all the others got a cap for every game, so they were a bit stingy that way. They were totally different from the way the other countries ran themselves.'

'I played five times, got one cap,' said Jimmy Murray. 'In fact, we never really got anything from the SFA over in Sweden. The Swedes gave us a piece of glass, a vase, and we had flannels and a blazer with the SFA badge on it, but that was it – nothing really to indicate that we'd ever been in Sweden.'

Looking at the half-bleached-out VHS of Scotland's final group game against France, it dawned on me that my father, contrary to what I'd always thought, hadn't brought home his shirt. The one upstairs in the attic had his usual number 11 on it. But during the World Cup players wore shirts bearing their squad numbers, and despite the poor quality of the recording the 21 on his back was clearly visible. Getting a shirt, it turned out, was more difficult in many ways than getting a cap. The latter were only rationed, the former completely forbidden. Mentioning it to members of the 1958 squad was lighting the blue touchpaper of 45-year-old grievances.

'You never got a shirt,' Alex Parker told me. 'Well I got one – against Hungary when we played them in Hungary. It was my first tour with Scotland and I hadn't got a jersey. I mentioned it to Tommy Doc who was my roommate. He says, "Don't worry Nosey" – he called me Nosey – "leave it to me," and he nicked one. It was a white one, funnily enough, and that was me.'

When Scotland lost 4–0 to England at Hampden in the April

before the World Cup, Jimmy Murray swapped his shirt with Bill Slater, the England wing-half, at the final whistle. 'When I got back into the dressing room Dawson Walker says, "Where's your jersey?" I says I've swapped it with Slater, he says, "Well you'd better go and get it then." So I had to go into the England dressing room – you can imagine how I'm feeling, getting whacked 4–0 – and ask him for my jersey back. It was a crazy situation. I got a white one in the end, you just had to stick it in your bag and hope you got away with it.'

My father had obviously done pretty well in managing to spirit away a blue one. I reckon it had to have been from the friendly against Hungary at Hampden Park, before the World Cup squad numbers were handed out and while he could still escape the Scotland party and head home with it.

So the shirt had been lying there all these years, preserving its navy blue in the dark of an attic trunk and declining to correct my assumption, maybe my decision, that it was a souvenir of my dad's World Cup. The truth was more interesting, and the story of how he'd managed to smuggle it out of Hampden would only have magnified its value. The shirt was one more exhibit that hadn't been called into evidence in time. Type another question in the unasked column and press the return key.

But we had known about the cap. The cap, at least, had been talked over while he was still alive, although it had taken the prospect of death to reveal its importance to him. It should really have been a moot point. Going back through the records, I could see that from the World Cup trials on 3 February 1958, until Scotland's elimination in the final group game against France on 15 June, my father had played in every Scotland game for which he'd been fit. Every game except the home international against England in April. If he'd played in that game he would have had his lone cap, tasselled and braided with the gold S v E, to back up his explanation to baffled

visitors as to why he didn't have any others. I can't find any defin-
itive explanation as to why he didn't play in that game. It may have
been because he'd cried off the previous Scotland fixture – the last
of the trial matches – with an injury. Or perhaps the selectors,
having already decided to take him to Sweden, wanted to use the
opportunity to take a look at Partick Thistle's Tommy Ewing, who
was doing his National Service and hadn't been available for the
trials. The following year, of course, there'd be the press outcry
about him being passed over for the same fixture, while he was
playing so well in Forest's cup run.

But the fact was, it hadn't happened. And for thirty-six years
it hadn't seemed to bother him, or at least he'd never mentioned
it. So what brought the issue to the surface in 1994? Perhaps it
was the sight of his two-year-old grandson starting to kick a small
ball in the back garden; the simultaneous reminder that his line
would go on and that he wouldn't. The cap would be something
to pass on to a boy who would naturally expect it to exist, as proof
and illustration of the stories that his father would tell him of his
own father.

And for himself too. He was sixty-two; retirement was looming,
the final acknowledgment that his achieving days were definitively
over and that it was all reminiscence from here on in. Perhaps he
didn't trust his memory, or felt that memory wasn't enough. But
then he didn't really reminisce. It wasn't in his make-up to rattle
on about the good old days. So maybe the pursuit of this piece of
unanswerable evidence was about him being able to remind himself,
quietly, without the fuss of having to remind anybody else.

The immediate trigger, though, was a reunion with some of the
surviving members of the 1958 World Cup squad. In March 1994,
Scotland were due to play the Netherlands in a friendly at Hampden
Park to mark the completion of the first phase of the stadium's
redevelopment. Not a gala occasion, but a good enough excuse to

see some of the old boys. My father was one of a large number of former internationals invited to the game. For the veterans of '58 the official letter from the Scottish FA must have had a nostalgic ring to it: '. . . with some regret the Association is unable to offset the various travel and hotel expenses which you may require to undertake.'

Over Scottish salmon, haggis and roast rib of Angus they talked about the state of the game, the state of their knees and probably how things might have been if John Hewie hadn't missed that penalty: *'Do you remember, the bloody thing bounced all they way up the field and they went and scored . . .'* It was more than likely: Jimmy Murray was at my dad's table, so was Alex Parker, and the Clyde full-back Harry Haddock – a great name in any sport – who had also been in the World Cup squad.

They all signed my dad's menu – perhaps he signed theirs – and underneath each name he printed in his own careful capitals the names of their respective clubs. Maybe he just wanted to be sure he could decipher the various scrawls and squiggles when he got home, but it's hard for me not to read it now as a sort of cataloguing exercise. It was a part of his personality; directly traceable, I suppose, to his father, the meticulous chronicler of car ownership and petrol prices. In the garage at home his nails and hinges and wood screws were all sorted into tiny drawers with handwritten labels. The same immaculate diagrams and notes that he used to record training routines were later applied to home-brewing projects and his own exercise regime; but he'd never bothered with his past before.

All the old internationals were presented with a commemorative medal by the Scottish FA to mark the occasion, a large embarrassed-looking disc in a blue plastic case that had the feel of a petrol station give-away. Perhaps it turned the conversation to real medals and to caps. Of his three teammates at the table, Jimmy Murray had played in the same two World Cup games as my father, Alex Parker had appeared in one and Harry Haddock not at all, but they all had caps — '*That's bad luck, eh, Stewart, to play in a World Cup and not play in a home international. Aye, there can't be many like you* . . .'

When he got home he wrote a letter to the Chief Executive of the Scottish Football Association, Jim Farry. In a gentle back-and-forth he respectfully asked and the SFA politely declined to award him a cap retrospectively. He was happy to reimburse them for the cost of having it made. They couldn't possibly make an exception. To do so would open the floodgates to further requests from other ex-internationals.

In fact, there were really no floodgates to open. True, the restrictions on Scotland caps had persisted, remarkably, until the mid-1970s, but the British Championship had been the mainstay of the domestic international season into the '80s. The number of players who had represented Scotland but somehow managed to avoid playing against England, Ireland or Wales was not going to constitute a torrent. In any case, the SFA didn't know because they kept no record. Jim Farry, though, was clear on his obligation to the traditions of Scottish football administration. To award a cap retrospectively 'would also demonstrate a lack of respect for the decisions of our predecessors at Park Gardens'.

My father seemed to let go of the idea. He'd tried, the SFA had been sympathetic, but their hands were tied. Honour seemed to have been satisfied and the issue faded away. Five years later the missing cap was invested with new importance when he was diagnosed with cancer. In March 2000 he tried again. Jim Farry had left the previous year but the reply – from the Assistant Director of Administration this time – was the same, sympathetic yet categoric: 'decisions not retrospective . . . place ourselves in a position . . . imagine the scenario . . . '

He wrote back offering to buy a blazer badge; they were sorry to say blazer badges were no longer available. This time he couldn't travel to the consolation game with France to mark the official inauguration of the new national stadium, he wasn't well enough. They sent him a pennant.

The idea of the cap became something of an obsession. He got it into his head that Ian St John was the man to help him. If my father could persuade Ian St John to highlight the injustice in his weekly column in Scotland's *Sunday Post*, he was sure he'd prevail. I don't know whether it was St John's stature within the game that my father thought might swing it for him, or the fact that he wrote in the *Sunday Post* – the paper of Oor Wullie and The Broons and all the homespun certainties of his childhood.

This kind of thing was my area of expertise. I could quite easily have made a couple of calls and interested someone in the story. At the same time I was a little uneasy about helping him to get publicity, because I knew he was torn: on the one hand he'd worked himself up into one of his lathers of conviction about his entitlement to the cap; on the other he didn't want to rock the boat and impugn the SFA in public. I told him I would make the calls if he wanted me to, but I could picture his annoyance when the story didn't appear exactly as he imagined it would – WORLD CUP VETERAN SLAMS SCOTLAND SCROOGES – and it began to dawn on him that he'd started a process he couldn't control. He said he'd stick with Ian St John. St John didn't call back.

In the meantime he confided in Dennis Marshall, his old friend from Nottingham. Conversations with Den tend to have the status of press releases, and a short time afterwards he was talking to Brian Tansley, the host of a show on BBC Radio Nottingham. He mentioned the story on air and again my father's agitation seemed to subside. He'd been given a public hearing and his claim had in some way been recognised.

In fact it had – not by the SFA, but by a family firm in Nottingham.

Brian Turner of Majestic Trophies had been a fourteen-year-old Forest fan in 1958. He and his wife Janet did some research and set about producing the most faithful replica they could of a Scotland cap: a tassel on the crown, gold braid around the peak, *J.J.S. Imlach, Scotland 1958* embroidered on the front panel above it. And instead of the initials of the old home international fixtures, the full names of his four opponents: v Hungary, Poland on one side; v Yugoslavia, France on the other. He was overwhelmed. The Turners were invited into the studio in Nottingham, my father, on the phone from Formby, could barely speak to thank them.

The story was picked up by the Nottingham *Evening Post*. In the pictures his pride and pleasure are almost unbearable to look at. I wanted to say, 'Dad, it's a fake.' A beautifully crafted, gold-tasselled, well-intentioned facsimile of the real thing, with all the same high-quality needlework and absolutely none of the significance. But his delight was deep and genuine, and who was I to puncture it by passing judgment.

The cap went into a glass-fronted cupboard in the hall where the wine glasses were kept, draped over a decanter. He wasn't allowed to drink by then, so there wasn't much chance of it being disturbed. Following in the first car behind the hearse, I could see it all the way to the crematorium, propped up against the coffin next to a Nottingham Forest team photo.

Later, I called around and discovered that two other members of Scotland's 1958 World Cup Squad had been in the same situation as my father. Archie Roberston of Clyde was dead; Hibs' Eddie Turnbull had never bothered pursuing the SFA for a cap. I was inclined to agree with Eddie's stoic acceptance of the rules as the rules, and the players simply victims of the period in which they'd played. Then I spoke to Tommy Docherty, who had gone on to manage the national team in the early '70s, and heard the story of how he'd intervened to help get a cap for Bob Wilson. Bob, he told me, had played for Scotland but never against the home countries.

What? The Scottish Football Association, with its fear of floodgates and its respect for tradition, had been dishing out retrospective caps on a selective basis? It was only Tommy Docherty's famous assertion that the best football managers are liars that kept me from calling Hampden Park there and then. Instead, I contacted Bob Wilson. He cautiously declared himself unaware of any intervention by Tommy Docherty on his behalf, but otherwise confirmed the story, which apart from the outcome sounded exactly like my father's. He'd written periodically to the SFA over the course of two decades with no success. It was only after Craig Brown took over as national manager that he'd got his cap. Jim Farry had also been helpful.

I mentioned this discovery to Eddie Turnbull. 'The English keeper? He got a cap? You're kidding.' He was scarcely less incredulous by the time I'd outlined the sequence of events to him. 'That's ridiculous. That takes some believing, that Wilson got a cap.'

To many people, Bob Wilson — born in Chesterfield and a key member of Arsenal's double-winning side of 1970–71 — was an English keeper and a very good one. In fact, he was perfectly well qualified to play for Scotland through his parents and turned out twice for the national team: in a European Championship qualifier against Portugal and a friendly against Holland, both in late 1971. His cap, inscribed with the initials P and H, finally arrived in 1996. That made it two years after Jim Farry had first written to my father, all sympathy and tied-hands, to say that it simply wasn't possible, and four years before the SFA — following 'some research into the circumstances' — had turned him down for a second time.

The implication was clear: a well-known, well-connected television presenter who could call on the Scotland manager to lobby on his behalf was worth an international cap in the eyes of the SFA; an older name from a less spotlit era, sitting at his dining-room table with a ballpoint pen and some Basildon Bond, could be safely fobbed off with the official line. I wondered how many others had received the same treatment as my father. And how many exceptions had been made. According to Craig Brown, Bob Wilson's wasn't the only one. But I only shared half of Eddie Turnbull's indignation, the half directed at the Scottish Football Association. I couldn't begrudge a cap to Bob Wilson, one of the game's few real gentlemen. If he qualified as a Scotland player – and there's absolutely no doubt that he did – then he was just as entitled to the recognition for it as anyone else. My father, for example.

In fact, I was grateful to Bob. He'd supplied me with the key to the floodgates. The men who ran the SFA, cornered by their own smug logic, couldn't possibly deny my dad a cap now. I could picture it arriving, needing to be signed for, a registered parcel of delayed vindication.

But I'd overestimated the bargaining power of the truth. In a tenth anniversary rematch of my father's original correspondence with them, the SFA refused to budge. The high-handedness which had helped create the fiasco of the 1958 World Cup was alive and well; faced with the evidence that would oblige them to give my father a cap, the SFA simply denied that the evidence existed. They could find no record in their archives of a cap being issued to Bob Wilson, so as far as they were concerned none had been. The facts didn't matter. I needn't bother waiting in for the postman.

For whose benefit had I been chasing it anyway? On whose behalf? I'd felt like it was something I could do for him, the least I could do for him, and I hadn't been able to. That's the story I had told myself. But he'd been happy with the copy. Maybe he was right to be, maybe it had more value: a cap crafted out of genuine feeling by people who saw him play and admired him, as opposed to an item squeezed out of an unwilling bureaucracy on a technicality — you broke the rules for someone else now break them for my dad — by a son who regretted not getting stuck in at the time.

Either way, the copy is the only one he ever wore.

'NOWADAYS, WE'RE BASICALLY ROOTIN' for jerseys.'

The speaker's own was fighting a battle on several fronts to contain him: a cheeseburger-built Buffalo Bills fan taking on the November wind-chill in his match-day uniform of team-replica shirt and construction worker's hard hat.

He leaned over the stand's perimeter wall towards the microphone, a partial eclipse with a beard. 'Seriously, what else is there? Players are just chasin' the money, teams threaten to leave every time a city won't come up with the dollars for a new stadium. So what's left? The jerseys. If you like a team's jersey colour, go root for 'em, y'know?'

I thanked him and moved along the sideline, grateful as always for the American football fan's facility in front of the camera. His performance sounded like it had been distilled from countless post-game rants in the local sports bar. He had a point, though, one I'd been pondering in various forms ever since I'd arrived in the country.

One of the chief attractions of life as a foreigner in America is this: it's not your fault. A Green Card, with its peculiar designation of 'Resident Alien', is essentially a guilt-free, access-all-areas pass to the best of both worlds. It allows you to indulge in all that's great about the self-proclaimed world's greatest country, while reserving your right to retreat to the sidelines at any moment and point – half shocked, half amused – at its worst excesses. And judgment delivered in a British accent carries its own implicit subtitles: 'Not my problem, mate – I didn't vote for any of this.'

Of course, American sport had been awash with money for decades before the tidal wave ever hit the UK, and entirely unapologetic about the fact. The question bothering the Buffalo Bills fan and seemingly quite a few of his compatriots was this: at what stage does sport become such big business that the original point is lost? At what dilution of cash to content can you no longer taste the sport in sport?

When millionaire players go on strike against millionaire team owners, depriving baseball fans of an entire season? When teams pack up and move, leaving their supporters behind, because they've had a better offer from another city in another state? When illiterate teenagers are given scholarships so that they can be put through the multimillion-dollar mincing machine of college football – then dumped out four years later still unable to read? When assaults, rapes and shootings are overlooked by college authorities because the perpetrators are valuable to the team? When high schools sack their coaches for having a losing season?

In 1989, when I'd first left the UK for America, the cash-fuelled soap opera that comes packaged with US sport had struck me as an entirely indigenous phenomenon, something which had no parallel at home. By the time I arrived back for good nearly a decade later, a transatlantic drift seemed to be underway. Granted, there were no PE teachers losing their jobs over a run of poor results by the under-15s, but the landscape was undoubtedly altered.

Many of the changes wrought by television and its money were clearly good for the game: fans better treated and better seated in front of a product of vastly improved, import-enhanced quality. The problem was, I couldn't seem to care that much about it. I'd still get caught up in the excitement of a good game if I happened to catch one, but – outside internationals and the few key fixtures that give a season its shape – the urge to catch one rarely took me. Worse than that, the stridency of the brash, relentless circus surrounding the game made it seem increasingly remote, like someone else's sport.

In America it really was someone else's sport and I could enjoy it on its own terms. I was thrilled and fascinated by the NFL, but I had no childhood pact with it. I carried no emotional baggage into Giants Stadium or Candlestick Park. So when Candlestick Park became 3Com Park to suit the sponsors, I could sympathise with the fans who'd been going there for years without feeling affronted personally. Flying from city to city, flashing my resident alien credentials, I was free to enjoy the plenty that was good about American sport. The rest was all context and flavour, part of the auxiliary narrative. Fascinating stuff – and not my fault.

In any case, the Americans – who after all had been richer longer – were much more at ease with their billions, and seemed to handle them more equitably. Football in the land of free enterprise was actually run as a cooperative – albeit a select and privileged one – with television and merchandising revenue split equally between all NFL teams.

There was a system of sharing out the best young players to try to head off the hegemony of a single superclub. Wage bills were capped at a figure set by the League for the same reason, and all player transactions were transparent: an athlete's agent earned money only from the athlete. In the land that invented the concept of good greed, charitable foundations were almost mandatory for any high-profile player. By comparison, football in the birthplace of the welfare state looked like dangerously leveraged Darwinism, with all the financial checks and balances of a gold rush.

The Yanks even seemed to work harder at our specialist subject, history. Perhaps because they had so little to start with, they went out of their way first to manufacture tradition, then to preserve it, with their Halls of Fame and annual induction ceremonies for the game's greats. Even their seemingly dry obsession with statistics had the effect of plaiting a long cord of numbers that ran through the decades connecting the modern game to its past. We had so much history we'd become cavalier about it. The arrival of the Premiership, with its empty columns of new all-time records waiting to be set, looked from a distance like football's Year Zero.

In the end, though, it wasn't to do with American sport. This wasn't a transatlantic face-off, it was something much closer to home. Perhaps it was just me. I'd finally grown out of football just as everyone else was growing into it. I'd missed the tastefully re-upholstered football special, powered by its Hornby engine and carrying implausible numbers of implausible fans (none of them admitting to having got on at the last stop). It had set off while I was away, and there was no catching up with it even if I'd wanted to. I'd been used to the role of outsider in the States, had enjoyed it. Now I felt like a stranger to my own game.

As it turned out, I wasn't entirely alone. Conversations with friends revealed a sort of non-specific unease about the brave new world of the Premiership. They were reluctant to mourn the loss of a connection with the past for its own sake; a break with tradition may be no bad thing if that tradition consists of standing to watch the game ankle-deep in a stream of other people's piss. Still, how do you passionately support a PLC? How do you maintain the undying devotion that makes you a fan when the club is doing its damnedest to turn you into a customer? One answer is that you simply blank it all out and focus on the team, on what happens out on the pitch. But what if the team is a rotating cast of millionaires with no more connection to your world than Tom Cruise, half of them here for no better reason than that the lira supply dried up in Serie A. What are you rooting for then?

In Italy, where football is anyway equal parts passion and cynicism, many fans simply declare themselves to be the club — after all they're the only constant — and everyone from the president to this year's crop of players merely their temporary representatives. They're as likely to abuse their own side as they are the opposition. The other reaction is a slow drift into the less intense life of the freelance fan: a soft spot for that club because they have this player; maybe tracking someone's career, changing allegiance when he moves; or deciding on the day, game by game, your loyalties up for grabs all the way through until kick-off. Hey, nice shirts . . .

Of course, the idea of clubs as friendly societies, functioning for the benefit of the fan, never existed outside cloth-capped, moist-eyed myth. Yet somehow it had been easier to suspend disbelief when the whole pantomime was a more modest, low-budget production; the villain a fat local butcher or car dealer, the players living up the road, not on another plane of existence altogether as they were now. The tacitly agreed fictions that had sustained the illusion of football as some sort of community, albeit a flawed one, seem to have been a function of scale. They couldn't survive enlargement. And, engorged as it was with money, the game was now very large indeed.

I still had one reason for keeping at least half an eye on the weekend's action: having something to say to my father during the weekly phone call home. The bulk of the conversation – weather, neighbours, family news – was with my mother, a Q & A routine of reassuring regularity which always finished the same way: 'Do you want a word with your dad? – Stewart!' While I was abroad it had been easy. I worked long hours at weekends and never knew the scores, so he was my results service. 'How did Everton get on . . . ? Who got the goal . . . ? Who got theirs . . . ?' I would ask him, and he'd talk me through it: 'cut in . . . edge of the box . . . just clipped it . . . top corner . . . keeper, no chance . . . tremendous . . . '

It was tremendous, a verbal sketch containing just enough structural information to enable me to add the colour and shading myself. Like baseball on the car radio, it was almost better than watching.

Baseball, though, was a foreign language, one in which I had to work at processing the cues into a serviceable picture: 'he winds . . . he deals . . . low and outside . . . full count . . .' When I phoned home I was listening to my native sporting dialect, a distant short-wave signal transmitted from childhood and still travelling, cutting through the crackle and cackle of all the American that was slowly annexing my sports vocabulary.

For most of the '90s, I suppose, this is how I followed football: kidding myself that I was still interested deep down, just unable to keep up with the game through distance, time zones, pressure of work. My last real show of active support came when Everton reached the FA Cup Final in 1995. None of the local sports bars in Atlanta was showing the game, but a six-pack persuaded one of the technicians at our post-production base to pull the pictures down off a passing satellite. They were fed through to the building's biggest television, in the boardroom, where I sat at the mahogany table with a takeaway breakfast and a dozen empty chairs for the 10 a.m. Eastern Time kick-off.

No studio pundits, no how-they-got-there, no Wembley Way; the pre-match build-up was a full-screen caption of transponder and co-ordinate details, which yielded worryingly late to mute pictures of the teams already out on the pitch. It was hardly a classic final. Still, I shouted and banged the table, an apoplectic chairman berating his minions to no effect. With the game itself silent, I was the only noise in the room. A security guard from reception put his head round the door.

'Sir, everything OK?'

'Yes, thanks, sorry.'

He didn't bother to come back when the goal went in.

Once I was home again in London, tuning in to watch seemed far more of an effort. On Sunday mornings I'd head out for the papers with a vague feeling of guilt at having no idea of the scores from the day before, or even what the fixtures had been. I'd skim the sports sections before I called home, not in order to pretend that I'd actually caught the highlights, just to make sure I had a list of prompts ready: 'I see we got beat again, eh, bloody hell . . . what was the Man U game like . . . what about Vieira, was it a sending off?' And he'd be away, nothing perfunctory about the answers, still full of passion and opinion.

Football's massive transformation hardly seemed to bother him. There was the occasional show of irritation – 'Pathetic!' – at some excess or other of the modern game, but he got much more worked up about yesterday's disallowed goal and that terrible tackle which had gone unpunished than any of what I thought of as the larger concerns.

The fact was, I'd lost the ability to see past the state of the game to the game itself. My father stared straight through it and saw what he'd always seen: the great first touch, the well-timed run, the perfectly judged ball to the far post, the reflex save. It was a passion he'd been born with, and he'd sustained it – it had sustained him – for the best part of seventy years. He'd handed it down to me and my brothers, and I'd mislaid it. Whose fault was that – mine, the game's, no one's in particular? I wasn't sure, but I knew it was something I couldn't tell him, any more than I could tell him that he was pretty much the only reason I still paid the game any attention at all.

In the later stages of his illness, when climbing the stairs required a stop halfway to regather his strength, television expanded to fill most of my father's horizon. On Sundays he'd sit half reclined in his chair like a man on a long-haul flight, and segue from the Premiership to the Nationwide, from Scotland to Spain and Italy, sidestepping the pre- and post-game blather that he detested as he went. Any gaps were plugged with golf.

It was into golf that he'd channelled all of his competitive energy once he was no longer playing football, and a fair proportion of it while he still was. In the early 1960s the Coventry *Evening Telegraph* ran a feature piece on my father which they illustrated with a family picture. In the photograph he is standing on the garden path with his bag of clubs over his shoulder, looking back at the group which has assembled on the front doorstep to wave him off. My older brother is holding a cap-gun and looks as though he's fidgeting to get back to whatever fiction he was acting out before being press-ganged into this one. My mother, pretending that stilettos and a pleated skirt were what she wore around the house every day, has me in her arms and is holding my hand up to wave to my departing father, no doubt at the photographer's request.

It's a fairly standard piece of stage-managed, provincial photo-journalism that just happened to capture a family truth. My mother spent most of her marriage waving my father off: away games, pre-season tours, exhibition matches, foreign competitions. And when he wasn't away with the boys playing football, he was away with them playing golf. Even in retirement he'd drive up to the golf club each morning, to potter about if not to play. She saw little more of him than when he'd been at the training ground every day. It was his last club, his last set of lads.

Formby Golf Club was both expensive and exclusive; the committee had reportedly turned down the chance to host the Open because they didn't want the intrusion. My father joined as an artisan member. The artisans were based in a brick bungalow that they'd built themselves behind a hedge in the corner of the car park, out of sight of the main clubhouse to which they weren't admitted. Working men, they were allowed onto the course at certain times and at reduced fees in return for performing a range of duties: divot replacement; green-sweeping at six o'clock on a Sunday morning.

As an adolescent I'd been indignant that this sort of forelock-tugging set-up still existed, and mortified that my father seemed happy to sign on for the tugging side. Surely he'd been through all this as a player, why on earth did he want to re-enact the whole business in his spare time?

To him it was perfectly straightforward: he wanted to play, and didn't want to pay the huge green fees. But it also meant that he was among his own. In the Scotland of his childhood, golf had been a working man's game: the spectacular links courses all municipal and populated by men off the trawlers, savouring the privilege of planting two feet on solid ground to sink a putt. Becoming a full member at Formby, which he could have done, would have been deserting the dugout for the directors' box. Not that he'd ever felt any sense of personal inferiority among the cigars and the cashmere coats, but he recognised the divide and knew which side of it he belonged. He made sure the main club knew it too. One of his proudest post-football achievements, alongside his hole-in-one, was captaining the artisans to victory in the President's Cup, the annual match against the full members.

It was his golfing companions who first realised something was wrong. He'd begun producing a sharp bark of pain on the follow-through to every shot. More than once they tried to persuade him to abandon a round and walk in – they'd take his clubs. He persevered, shouting his way round the course for several weeks until it became too much. The pain was damage to his spine and ribcage. He had multiple myeloma, cancer of the bone marrow, and the disease was dissolving the calcium from his skeleton, making it brittle. Each swing of the club was an attack on his own bones. By the time the diagnosis was eventually made, chronic had become acute. In the space of a week he jumped a generation, from a fit 67-year-old to a fragile grandfather figure. He seemed to have shrunk. In fact he'd collapsed, his spine compacting like an inexpertly dynamited chimney.

Through sheer force of will, and to a mixed reception of admiration and horror, he resumed driving. But the list of things he could do for himself was being systematically scored through, an item at a time to start with, then in categories, until finally, and for the first time in his life, he was a spectator.

The last game my father and I watched together was in September 2001, England's 5–1 win over Germany in the World Cup qualifiers. Trips and phone calls home were much more frequent by then, and his health had forced its way onto the shortlist of conversational topics. Conversation, though, was briefer than usual; all his resources now seemed to be focused inwards on the illness, and he couldn't stand too much noise or activity around him. Even a visit from his grandson, a lively nine-year-old on whom he doted, was sometimes too much. But on this Saturday afternoon it was just the two of us, a pair of England fans braced for the disappointment promised by the traditional fixture with Germany. My father was never an anti-Sassenach Scot. He'd had an entire playing career in England, a wife and three English sons; rooting for the auld enemy came naturally.

When England took the lead just before half-time I leaped out of my chair and turned to see him wincing in his. He shrugged it off, but I could see that any pleasure he'd taken in the goal had been drowned out by the shock to his system from my celebration of it. He had enough going on internally without having to absorb sudden bursts of loud and unexpected sensory information from outside. I sat back down. The second half was a massively enjoyable, if slightly surreal, affair. As the score mounted and the tumult built in Munich's Olympic Stadium, we sat like two light-opera enthusiasts, greeting each goal with polite and restrained rapture.

*   *   *

A month later I watched the decisive qualifying game against Greece on my own. It was ninety minutes' relief in the middle of a there-and-back trip to London from Formby to pick up my suit for the funeral. For a moment I'd thought of grabbing it when I'd got the call from the hospital the previous Monday evening, but it would have seemed a betrayal, as though I'd lost faith in him. After the late-night drive up the motorway I'd found him awake and alert at 3 a.m. on the quietly pulsing critical-care ward. 'There's been a bit of a fracas,' he said.

My mother, forever balancing her own levels of concern with his vehement reluctance to go to hospital, had called an ambulance some time after ten. Their next-door neighbour, a lay preacher, had followed behind in his own car and, when the time seemed to have come, administered the last rites. As he finished he was alarmed to hear a murmured reply. 'Thanks, John,' my father had said opening his eyes, 'I enjoyed that.'

The next day was one of his best for a long time. My mother and I visited him in the morning and said we'd be back later that afternoon. When we got there he was fuming. Dwarfed by the dimensions of the high-backed armchair at the side of the bed, he perched like a miniature pontiff. There'd been a misunderstanding over the time and he'd been waiting for what he thought was hours. For once, his obsessive clock-watching seemed perfectly understandable. His mood quickly brightened, though, and as we left for the evening he gestured towards us from his chair: 'You are absolved.'

When the midnight call came from the hospital this time the drive was only twenty minutes. My mother, worried about the police cameras, warned me not to speed. Before we could see him we were shown into a side room. The consultant wanted permission to turn off the machinery keeping my father alive. 'But this happened last night and by the time I got here he was sitting up in bed,' I told the doctor. That wasn't going to happen this time. My mother made the decision, and with Steve, who'd had a longer drive from the Wirral, we sat round the bed to cheer him on. It was the only time I'd ever really watched my father, been there to encourage him and urge him forwards. Now that there was no chance of real recovery, just ever more painful delay, dying seemed like a positive act, something he could do for himself. We were ranged round the rectangle of the bed like fans to make sure he didn't falter. This was something he knew how to do, perform under the pressure of expectation; we were improvising.

The awful temptation of a modern death is to pay attention to the flow of medical information instead of the ebbing life in front of you. He was being counted out by the heart-rate monitor in ever lengthening pauses, each one of them indistinguishable from the beginning of unbroken silence, until the green screen pinged and peaked and the next pause began. The critical-care nurses, their ears tuned to pick the approaching death march out of this toneless electronica, moved in to switch it off and spare us the last few notes.

'Did you ever see him play?' I was asked a number of times at the funeral reception. It was my job to carry round the worn leather box containing his medal for anyone who wanted to see it. No, I wanted to say, but at least I was there to see him off. At least I started paying attention before it was too late, even if it was only by minutes.

Almost the entire practical business of bereavement was taken care of from within the artisans' brick bungalow. The undertaker was a man whose membership application my father had vetted, giving his approval only after an eighteen-hole test of ability and sportsmanship, the minister at the funeral was a regular playing partner. A couple of days after the service, eight or ten of them walked out with us to scatter his ashes at the seventeenth, which was as far onto the course as his stamina would take him when he could no longer play, and where he'd stand to welcome the lads in towards the end of their round.

Epilogue:
Homecoming

RETRACING THE ROUTE. IT looked easy enough on the Nottingham *A–Z*: a spiralling sweep of the finger from the Midland Station, where the team had stepped off the train, to the Council House building in Market Square; five minutes' walk away, or a triumphant hour and a half by open-top bus.

Armed with the homecoming parade itinerary from the Nottingham *Evening Post* of Monday 4 May 1959, I parked in one of the grim side streets that attach themselves to train stations. As I got out of the car, I saw that what had looked like a junk shop as I'd driven past was actually a shabby football memorabilia place. It seemed like a good sign, which was more than could be said for the sign itself: 'Programme World' – the words were arched over a grimy globe – and underneath 'Est. 1978, Anything To Do With Football, The Older The Better'. There were a couple of small bikes for sale outside – possibly the authentic childhood property of Nigel Clough or Garry Birtles. In the window was an assortment of videos and a Manchester United table lamp.

'1959 Cup Final? No, duck. We might have one or two bits, but I wouldn't know where to start.' From the tone of the woman behind the counter I understood that starting was not something she undertook lightly, and certainly not for just anyone who walked in off the street. I headed to the station.

At the London Road railway bridge near the Eastcroft depot, children hung over the parapet in an attempt to get a glimpse of the team as their train pulled in from London.

That would have been my father's first hint of the reception awaiting him and his teammates. The station looks now pretty much as it did then. The platforms have tented wooden roofs painted white like marquees for a summer fête. The structural support is all I's and T's and X's of Derby steel in dark gloss. As they arrived they'd have passed under the boxed-in footbridge that connects the platforms, with its lattice of supporting struts, like a row of kisses, or a filled coupon.

Hundreds saw the team arrive at the Midland Station two minutes early – at 6.19 p.m. They were welcomed by stationmaster Mr Gordon Rogers wearing top hat and tails for this special occasion.

The tour began five minutes ahead of the 6.45 schedule. Small children on Queen's Drive used the playing field swings to get their only possible view of the team.

I was really taken by the image of these children, hopelessly blocked by the backs of adults six deep at the roadside, then suddenly appearing above them at the apex of their swing for a split-second's grandstand view, the parade going by as a sequence of snatched stills. But the Queen's Drive swings were gone, along with the tall gabled boarding houses where people had hung out of the windows to see the players pass by. It's an ugly dual carriageway now with little to see; a few light industrial units and a Porsche garage with a well-stocked forecourt, where the '59 team's modern-day equivalents might window-shop over the heads of the crowd.

Forest's wasn't the classic open-top bus – the Corporation hadn't been able to find one – it was a single-decker coach with two cut-outs in the roof. My father was at the back, in the slipstream of the continuous cheer breaking ahead of him over the figurehead of Jack Burkitt who, in photographs at least, hadn't let go of the Cup since he'd left the Royal Box.

In Carlton Road near the Corporation transport depot one supporter was watching the parade who had never seen the Forest team in person. He was 19-year-old Brian Cole, a cripple who was wheeled to his vantage point in an invalid carriage by friends two hours before the procession was due to pass.

He waited patiently for the heroes he had seen only on a television screen. 'I should like to get Stewart Imlach's autograph,' he told our reporter, 'but I don't suppose the coach will stop.'

The transport depot where Brian Cole had sat waiting for my father is dwarfed by the National Ice Centre, and the traffic runs four lanes wide in the opposite direction to the route of the homecoming parade. I stood with my back to the posters advertising Atomic Kitten and Barney's World and squinted at him across the road.

On a side street just off Carlton Road was the Euro Sports Bar – 'All Major Live and Exclusive Events Shown on the Big Screen'. I imagined the customers nipping outside with their drinks for a quick look as the coach passed, then ducking back inside to check that it was really happening, on one of the three large projection screens. On this afternoon Manchester United and Southampton were being ignored by fewer than a dozen customers. A couple of hyperactive kids zoomed between the tables while their parents ate lunch surrounded by carrier bags. Saturday was shopping day.

On the walls was an interior designer's sporting iconography: giant blow-ups of Ali landing a punch on Frazier, and the Grand National field clearing Becher's. The football pictures weren't as big but there were more of them: Pelé and Bobby Moore swapping shirts at the 1970 World Cup in Mexico; Maradona using the hand of God to beat Peter Shilton when the competition returned there sixteen years later. Domestic football was represented by Vinnie Jones and Paul Gascoigne, frozen together as scrotum-grabber and grabbee, long before Jones turned his thuggery into celebrity and

Gazza's talent for the game was undone by his lack of talent for life outside it.

Things could have been worse – a US theme with baseball uniforms and NBA vests in glass cases – still, it was a depressingly off-the-peg decor. We could have been anywhere. Nearer the bar, away from the prime wall-space and well down the scale of print sizes, there were nods towards history and geography: a fish-eye shot of the City Ground and a signed picture of the Brian Clough-era Forest team. Nothing from 1959. I headed back out to rejoin the parade route.

In the long Alfred Street men had climbed hoardings to get a vantage view of their heroes. Alfred Street primary school yard was full of children as though it was playtime during school hours.

One of the most impressive home-made banners was that of Miss Evelyn Cox of 100 Alfred Street South. A keen Forest supporter, she spent all day on Sunday embroidering the names of the whole team on a piece of white silk which read 'Welcome To The Merry Men'.

The Coxes were long gone from Alfred Street. In fact, Alfred Street was only barely hanging on itself: concrete bollards and child-friendly pedestrian zones had split it into three non-contiguous stretches. Forest's homecoming parade route had been town-planned out of existence. I pressed on, sticking as close to the line of yellow-highlighter on my *A–Z* as the dead ends and diversions allowed.

Banners with the paint still wet were being waved in the boulevards. Saucepans and frying pans were being beaten from the upstairs windows of many of the flats.

At the top of Mansfield Road three men played loud and long on four-foot hunting horns. A coach from Hull had been halted by the crowds and the occupants – all women – were cheering as loudly as anyone.

Alfred Street, in fact most of the route to this point, had been working class. On the climb up to Mansfield Road, the terraces disappeared and the houses, and the spaces between the houses, grew bigger. Now, these handsome villas would be well within the budget of Forest's first-team personnel, even if they might be a little staid or too close to town; then, they would have been the preserve of committee members, or the manager.

From the top of the hill the coach, with a rear escort of fans on bikes and on foot, started a wide anticlockwise loop downwards, back into the city centre.

At the foot of Derby Road a 25-piece brass band swung onto the head of the procession. It was the Bestwood Black Diamonds, one of whose members, Norman Brown, had sat up into the early hours of the morning writing out the band parts to the Robin Hood theme tune from memory.

In Lenton Boulevard rosettes the size of dinner plates were worn, and schoolgirls who had never before used lipstick in their lives put some on to match the Forest rosettes on their dresses.

Several parents had dressed their children in South Sea Garlands of red and white tissue paper . . . cats with ribbons round their necks were clutched by their young owners. The team were greeted by a bevy of monster balloons painted with brilliant slogans by Mr W. Storey and waved by his wife and three little girls. 'Actually I don't really care to watch football myself,' Mr Storey told a reporter. 'I would rather just listen to it on the radio.'

This was a community event that involved the whole community, like a royal jubilee; it wasn't just about football. Two hundred thousand people had turned out to honour eleven of their own, men who would eventually be absorbed back into the crowd when their time was up. Not yet though. The future prison officers, publicans, social workers and groundsmen smiled and waved at a multiplied mirror image of themselves slipping by in second gear. Up at the front, the man behind the counter at the post office still held onto the cup.

Epilogue

The procession swept down Long Row into the square, the loudspeakers started to play Robin Hood and the crowd exploded into a roar of welcome that drowned out every other sound.

Policemen joined arms and tried to keep back the hordes of people as they surged forward towards the centre of the square. People leaped on the traffic island in Long Row to escape the crush.

My father would have recognised people on his way round. The crowd was huge, but Nottingham wasn't. The bus had already made one unscheduled stop; my mother had told the driver where she'd be standing, holding Steve up to wave. By now she was inside the Council House, where there was going to be a civic dinner once the team arrived. Still, there would have been friends and neighbours shouting to him from the roadside, and the height of the coach kept the players close enough to the crowd to make out individual faces. Chic Thomson spotted his father, who was supposed to be back at home in Perth, standing on a bollard in Market Square.

I parked as close as I could and approached the square on foot. It's the heart of the city's shopping area; I must have gone there as a child with my mother. But it was years since I'd been back to Nottingham, and if I'd ever stood in front of the Council House I hadn't connected it to the Cup Final.

It was a standard Saturday afternoon scene: shoppers, teenagers gathered in small groups, a couple of skateboarders. Nobody was paying me any attention, why should they be? Still, for some reason I felt self-conscious. Then I realised – and I'm not sure how I'd managed to keep the information from myself all the way round the route – that I was about to imitate my father, take up his position on the left of the twin line of players that I'd seen in the photographs and walk down into the sunken central plaza as he had to, the stereo roar from the massed banks of fans on either side.

While the Forest players stepped down from the coach, ambulance men and police officers carried fainting women and children to safety as they collapsed against the railings. The St John ambulance brigade with 28 members on duty in the square reported over 50 cases of people fainting in the crowd.

I took my hands out of my pockets. In the pictures he looks as though he's marching . . . Christ, surely I wasn't really about to do this.

Just then, I registered something out of the corner of my eye, on one of the cast-iron municipal rubbish bins dotted round the square. I seized on the distraction – anything to delay this ludicrous commemorative fifty-yard walk – and as I recognised the familiar crest, it struck me for the first time that Nottingham and its team shared a coat of arms. The team of my dad's era that is; sometime in the 1970s the club adopted a cartoon Sherwood Forest oak as its logo. But the city's had never changed and, now that I'd noticed it, I suddenly had the impression that the whole town centre had been branded by the '59 Cup Final team, rather than the other way round. The bin, the bus shelters, the pavement in front of the Council House itself all bore the team crest: twin stags supporting a red shield with a walled castle above. Beneath it was the motto that they also shared, and which I'd never before stopped to read. My Latin isn't up to much, but it didn't need to be: *Vivit Post Funera Virtus* – Virtue Lives on after Death.

In the right frame of mind, you can find special meaning in the contents of a fortune cookie, or a Christmas cracker, but Virtue Lives on after Death? That wasn't a civic motto, it was a family one, a tombstone inscription. From Cornwall to Caithness, there's no county or city or borough council with anything remotely as personal. Take a look sometime: they're all industry and prosperity and marching forward together. Virtue Lives on after Death. I felt slightly concussed.

In the distance I could hear a football crowd singing, getting closer. This was too much. Being sucker-punched by the street furniture was one thing; auditory hallucinations were beyond a joke. I turned towards the sound and saw a group of Notts County fans enter the square, loudly differentiating themselves from the rest of the Saturday afternoon crowd as they cut a path through the city centre on their way to Meadow Lane. They weren't there to provide a soundtrack to my sentimental journey, they were giving the full treatment to that old terrace standby sung to the tune of 'Land of Hope and Glory': 'We hate Nottingham Forest . . .'

There was no maintaining the portentous mood after that, thank God. I did the walk anyway – more of an amble in the end, nobody watching would have wondered what I was up to – and stood beneath the grand façade of the Council House, looking up at the balcony where my father stood with his teammates to greet the crowd.

By then the first few of the thousands began to drift away up the surrounding streets saying, 'Well, I saw them.'

Postscript

In February 2006, following a campaign which attracted the support of leading figures in Scottish football, the SFA issued a posthumous cap to Stewart Imlach, and to more than eighty other Scotland internationals who had never received one.

Acknowledgments

I am indebted to many people for their time and their help in the researching of this book:

Lossiemouth: Johnny Archibald, Joe Campbell, Robbie Campbell, Jimmy George, Sandy Reid, David Stewart, Donnie Stewart, May and Slater Scott, Colin Tough, Robert Weir

Bury: Les Bardsley, Peter Cullen, Tom Daniel, Cyril Fairclough, John Forrest, Enid Gleadall, Dave Hatton, Eric Massey, Richard and Eleanor Vipond

Derby: Bert Mozley, Terry Webster

Nottingham Forest: Eddie Baily, Les Bradd, Hazel Burkitt, Jimmy Linton, May McKinlay, Nottingham Forest Football Club, John Quigley, Karl Pridmore, Ken Stevenson, Brian Tansley, Geoff and Rita Thomas, Chic and Pat Thomson, Mike Tinkley, Jack Wheeler, Jeff and Nell Whitefoot

Luton: Seamus Dunne, Ken Hawkes, Albert McCann, Brendan McNally, Dave Pacey

Coventry: Dickie Dowsett, Lol Harvey, Jimmy Hill, Mick Kearns, Brian Nicholas

Crystal Palace: Bill Glazier, Dick Graham, John Jackson, Terry Long, George Petchey, Reverend Nigel Sands, David Selby, John Sewell, Roy Summersby, Jess Willard

Scotland: Craig Brown, Danny Burn, Eric Caldow, Doug Cowie, Bob Crampsey, Tommy Docherty, John Hewie, Jim Hossack, Graham Leggat, Dave Mackay, Robert McElroy, Jimmy Murray,

Alex Parker, Eddie Turnbull, Brian and Janet Turner, Ian Wheeler, Bob Wilson, Fraser Wishart

Everton: Erlend Clouston, John Connolly, Jack Connor, Martin Dobson, Ronnie Goodlass, Darren Griffiths, Colin Harvey, Chris Hassell, Eric Harrison, Howard Kendall, Brian Labone, Jim McGregor, Dave Prentice, Ian Ross

PFA: Carol Brown, Gordon Taylor

BBC: Peter Dimmock, Chris Graham

Formby Artisans: Bill Caunt, Ken Jones

Historical detail: John Harding, Andy Ward

More than anyone else outside my family, Dennis Marshall was an inexhaustible source of information and advice. John Pawsey got the book off the ground. Tristan Jones got it into shape. Matt Rendell set the standard, then did his best to help me match it. Finally, thanks go to my brothers, Steve and Mike, and most of all, with love, to my mother, Joan.

For permission to reproduce previously published and unpublished material, the author and publishers make grateful acknowledgment to: Guardian Newspapers Limited (Don Davies' Manchester United vs. Nottingham Forest match report © Guardian Newspapers Limited 1957); Nottingham Forest Football Club (Stewart Imlach's contract); and the Nottingham *Evening Post* (May 1959 homecoming report). For permission to reproduce photographs the author and publishers make grateful acknowledgement to: Bolton Evening News (*p.3*), Bury Times (*p.3*), The Scottish Daily Express (*p.4, p.5, p.6, p.7*), Nottingham Post Group Ltd (*p.8, p.12*), Barratts/ALPHA/EMPICS (*p.13*), Daily Mail (*p.7*). Every effort has been made to trace or contact all copyright holders, and the publishers will be pleased to correct any omissions brought to their notice at the earliest opportunity.